Issues

6   Preface
8   What is interior design?
14 A brief history of the profession
20 Interior design and education
24 Interior sensibility
26 Cross-disciplinary concerns
28 Adaptation
32 Restoration, preservation, conservation
36 Found objects
42 Sustainability
46 Details
50 Surfaces
54 Representation and communication

Anatomy

60 Anatomy

62 Strategy
64 Strategy: responsive interiors
66 Strategy: responsive home interiors
70 Strategy: responsive work interiors
72 Strategy: responsive culture interiors
78 Strategy: responsive knowledge interiors
84 Strategy: responsive retail interiors
88 Strategy: autonomous interiors
90 Strategy: autonomous home interiors
92 Strategy: autonomous work interiors
100 Strategy: autonomous culture interiors
104 Strategy: autonomous knowledge interiors
108 Strategy: autonomous retail interiors

112 Tactics
114 Tactics: responsive interiors
116 Tactics for responsive interiors: light
120 Tactics for responsive interiors: objects
124 Tactics for responsive interiors: plane
128 Tactics for responsive interiors: surface
134 Tactics: autonomous interiors
136 Tactics for autonomous interiors: light
140 Tactics for autonomous interiors: objects
144 Tactics for autonomous interiors: plane
148 Tactics for autonomous interiors: surface

Portfolios

152   Portfolios

154   Tarruella & Lopez
160   Randy Brown Architects
168   Pugh + Scarpa Architects
174   Multiplicity
182   Merkx + Girod
188   Universal Design Studio
194   Agence Andrée Putman
200   David Archer Architects
206   David Collins Studio
212   Ben Kelly Design
218   Clive Wilkinson Architects
224   Casson Mann
230   Lazzarini Pickering Architetti
238   Gensler
244   Land Design Studio

Etcetera

250   Bibliography
252   Glossary
254   Index
256   Credits

Preface

What is Interior Design? serves as an introduction for students, academics, and practitioners who have an interest in interior architecture, interior design, interior decoration, and building reuse. The book will examine the fundamental characteristics of interior space, including the nature and qualities of organizing an interior space, an understanding of the material and surface qualities of found and applied textures, and the analysis and understanding of existing buildings. As well as discussing the theoretical issues underpinning the design of interior space, this book will also contextualize the current issues within education and practice, and will examine historical and contemporary concerns in design. The final part of the book looks at the work of current international practitioners, who are operating in all of the different realms of the design of interior space.

Interior design has often been regarded as a superficial practice that lacks any particular set of distinct theories or principles. Yet the study and practice of designing interior space is evolving as an independent, intellectual subject that is far beyond the cosmetic concerns of television makeover shows. Interior architecture, interior design, interior decoration, and building reuse are very closely linked subjects, all of which deal, in varying degrees, with the transformation of a given space, whether that is the crumbling ruin of an ancient building or the drawn parameters of a new building proposal. This alteration or conversion leads to a complex process of understanding the qualities of the given space, while simultaneously combining these factors with the functional requirements of new users. This distinctive attribute creates a unique set of issues, theories, and processes that are different to many other design practices, yet in places these overlap with other disciplines, such as installation art and architecture.

At the beginning of the twenty-first century, there is a definite rise in the number of interior practitioners and architects who are tackling interior projects, whether building adaptation or true interior design. The popularity of interior design education, at both undergraduate and postgraduate level, has never been higher. Despite this, there is still very little legislation or definition around this subject, and few publications of any academic substance that investigate the subject's issues, processes, and theories. The exponential growth of the provision of courses, and the lack of critical substance in this field, needs to be addressed. It is apparent that answers to the questions of how distinct the subject is, what is its own history, what are the particular ideologies and principles of its education, and who are the key practitioners in the field, are long overdue.

This book aims to address all of these concerns.

**Casa da Música,
Porto, Portugal**
Design: OMI Architects. The vertical circulation in this building is realized as an exciting journey around the central auditorium. The interior is a composite of ideas and construction that are elegantly combined in this modern concert hall.

What is interior design?

The design of the interior is an extremely distinct subject that differs from almost every other design discipline. The interior is bound to its situation; it is enclosed within a building, which is, in turn, contained within its context. The question of the existing is central to the design process. The particular location of the interior has an influence upon the design that often far outweighs other considerations. Other design genres, such as graphics, fashion, or industrial design, have to consider the function, the aesthetic qualities, and the structure of a piece. The interior designer must consider these aspects too, but they also have to respond to the particular place that the interior inhabits. The interior can become part of the place; it can assemble meaning and also

Opposite: Virgin Atlantic lounge, Heathrow Airport, London, UK
Design: Softroom Architects. The language of an interior is one of the most important considerations in the design process. This airport lounge creates a soothing preflight environment while also evoking the dynamics of flight inside the airport terminal.

Below: Turning the Place Over, Liverpool, UK
Design: Richard Wilson. Site-specific installations create an intimate relationship between art and location. In Liverpool the sculptor Richard Wilson has changed this existing building so that it can be reread in a new way.

Above: Givenchy boutique, Paris, France
Design: Jamie Fobert Architects. Specialisms such as exhibition, workplace, retail, leisure, and domestic design characterize the practice of interiors. In this boutique the exquisite clothing is displayed in freestanding boxes. These are clad in glass on the outside while the interior is finished in traditional wood paneling, representing the two faces of the Givenchy brand.

Left: Lotus furniture, Venice, Italy
Design: Zaha Hadid Architects. Elements and objects are essential components of the interior. Their organization, detail, and scale populate space and usually accommodate function. At the Venice Architecture Biennale, the designer displayed furniture prototypes that blurred the boundary between object and enclosure.

give value and consequence to a situation. Perhaps only installation art and architecture, both subjects that interiors are closely related to, are so closely associated with their individual location.

The much-quoted maxim from Vitruvius: "Commodity, firmness, and delight" is fundamental to all architectural and interior design. Commodity expresses the functionality of the object; does it work? Is it fit for purpose? Firmness describes the structural integrity of the piece; will it stand up and what is it made from? Has it the strength to do its job? Can it support itself and anything else that it is designed to hold? Delight asks whether the element has an aesthetic value; is it beautiful? Is it striking? Is it visually appealing? The designer's search to fulfill the expectations of this aphorism can be applied to every type of interior space and

the objects that inhabit it. Traditionally the subject has been associated with interior design/decoration and has been seen as peripheral to the essential subject of architecture. The reuse of existing buildings is a subject that is central to the evolution of the urban environment and issues of conservation and sustainability have become vital to the development of cities. As the approach to the design and use of the urban environment has changed, so the prevailing attitude toward building reuse has also altered. Therefore interior design has emerged as an area of interest in its own right, rather than an adjunct of architecture or an expansion of surface decoration.

The study of interior architecture, design, and decoration is growing as an intellectual discipline, but it is one that is so often dogged with issues of decorative finishes and cut MDF. Interiors are frequently regarded as the forgotten elements within a much larger theoretical discussion, as the spaces left over and produced very much as a consequence of building exterior. At the beginning of the twenty-first century, the design of the interior is beginning to be regarded as a subject rich in history and theory, which can have a beneficial influence upon the manner in which space is occupied.

Interior design is a term that has traditionally been used to describe all types of interior projects, encompassing everything from decoration to remodeling. However, in view of the fact that building reuse has become such a highly regarded practice, it has clearly become necessary to divide the main subject and define more clearly the individual specialisms.

This would be a good point to clarify the precise nature of each area. The exact disciplines inevitably overlap, but by and large the differences seem to concern the magnitude of change to the occupied space.

Interior decoration is the art of decorating interior spaces or rooms to impart a particular character that functions well with the existing architecture. Interior decoration is concerned with such issues as surface

Tourisms: SuitCase Studies, traveling exhibition
Design: Diller Scofidio + Renfro. In this exhibition, 50 identical suitcases held exhibits from locations across the USA, with each one showing tourist attractions from each place. The cases can be packed up and then shipped to the next exhibition location.

pattern, ornament, furniture, soft
furnishings, lighting, and materials.
It generally deals only with minor structural
changes to the existing building. Typical
examples of this practice are the design of
domestic, hotel, and restaurant interiors.
Interior design is an interdisciplinary practice
that is concerned with the creation of a
range of interior environments that articulate
identity and atmosphere through the
manipulation of spatial volume, placement
of specific elements and furniture, and
treatment of surfaces. It generally describes
projects that require little or no structural
changes to the existing building, although
there are many exceptions to this. The
space is retained in its original structural
state and the new interior inserted within it.
It often has an ephemeral quality and
typically would encompass such projects as
retail, exhibition, and domestic interiors.

Interior architecture is concerned with the
remodeling of existing buildings and attitudes
toward existing spaces and structures,
building reuse, and organizational principles.
It bridges the practices of interior design and
architecture, often dealing with complex
structural, environmental, and servicing
problems. This practice encompasses a huge
range of project types from museums,
galleries, and other public buildings, through
office and other commercial buildings to
domestic developments.

These are the three distinct areas.
Each practice has certain distinctive
characteristics, and yet they all overlap:
they possess a close connection in their
interaction with the existing space.

**Queen Mary Medical
School Library,
London, UK**
Design: Surface Architects.
Interior projects will often
involve the reuse of old
buildings. In this project,
the designers installed a
new element to facilitate the
functioning of the library.
The contemporary language
of the installation contrasts
with the stonework of the
existing building.

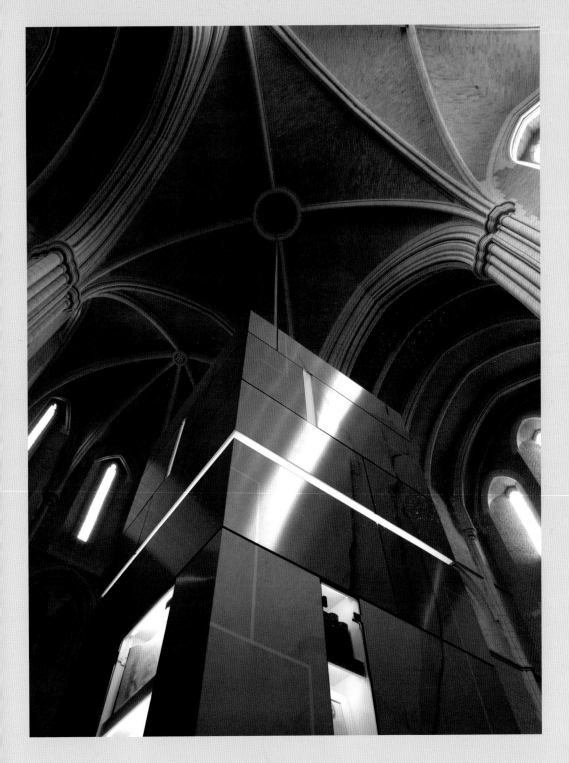

A brief history of the profession

Interior design is a relatively new profession. That is not to say that the art of interior design/decoration/architecture has only recently been practiced, it was just not regarded as a distinct and particular subject. Traditionally the upholsterer or furniture maker offered advice on the decoration and arrangement of the house, or the architect would assume control over the design of the complete building, inside and out.

The profession of the interior decorator emerged in the early twentieth century. Initially, enthusiastic amateurs were responsible for the rise in its popularity.

The decoration of the domestic dwelling was considered to be the role of the woman, and it was their gradual emancipation that first promoted the subject as a viable profession for females. Inspired by the suffragette movement, traditional family roles were changing, allowing some women to establish economic independence. It was considered respectable and suitable to be a consultant on the organization and decoration of domestic environments.

At the turn of the twentieth century, new wealth created a class of rich patrons who, in a desire to express their affluence,

Left: Apsley House, London, UK
Design: Robert Adam. The interior and the exterior, that is, the building and rooms, have been conceived as a whole entity, which unites structure and space with furniture and decoration.

Right: Victor Horta House and Studio, Brussels, Belgium
Design: Victor Horta. Structure, lighting, furniture, and surfaces are all carefully considered and elegantly designed in the dining room of this house.

employed designers to extensively rework their homes. Notable practitioners at this time were Elsie de Wolfe, Lady Sibyl Colefax, Edith Wharton, Ogden Codman, Dorothy Draper, and the Herter brothers. As well as work on private residences, other projects that were deemed suitable included ladies' and gentlemen's clubs and other social spaces where the rich gathered to entertain and be entertained. The decorator would coordinate and control furniture, textiles, color, and light to create lavish backdrops for large social gatherings.

The publication of books such as *The House in Good Taste* (1913) by Elsie de Wolfe and *The Decoration of Houses* (1897) by Edith Wharton and Ogden Codman also served to popularize the profession and to characterize the work of interior decorators as a separate professional entity from the upholsterers and scenic painters who came before them. Wharton and Codman were probably the first to use the term "interior architect" in *The Decoration of Houses*:

"A building, for whatever purpose erected, must be built in strict accordance with the requirements of that purpose. Its decoration must harmonize with the structural limitations (which is by no means the same thing as saying that all decoration must be structural), and from this harmony of the general scheme of decoration with the building, and of the details of the decoration with each other, springs the rhythm that distinguishes architecture from construction. Thus all good architecture and good decoration (which it must never be forgotten, is only interior architecture) must be based on rhythm and logic."

Throughout the twentieth century, many designers used the title "interior decorator," and although some were acting purely as decorators, others were involved in much more substantial projects. For example, the prolific British designer of the interwar period, Robert Atkinson, is best known for the flamboyant art deco interior of the Daily Express Building in Fleet Street, London, completed in 1932. The glorious blue and gold mosaic interior complements, and is totally appropriate within, the steel and glass building. This is much more than a decorative project, it is an interpretative design. However, the minimalist interiors of modernism left little space for interpretation, or often, any sort of intervention at all. Architects such as Adolf Loos and Le Corbusier conceived their interiors as integral to the building; they were also stripped bare of any superfluous ornamentation or decoration. Many of the early projects of Adolf Loos could be regarded as interior design or even

American Bar,
Vienna, Austria
Design: Adolf Loos. The claustrophobic quality of this tiny space is alleviated by the mirrored cornice above the timber wainscot of the bar, a device that reflects a seemingly endless interior.

adaptation rather than true architecture, and he was instrumental in popularizing the subject in his early projects and his writings for the newspaper *Das Andere*.

Le Corbusier's design for the Beistegui apartment in Paris—a rooftop remodeling that was designed to resemble a sleek, oceangoing liner—had an interior that was designed to represent a surrealist salon. But the interior, by Emilio Terry, is rarely mentioned in discussions about the building, highlighting the dislocation and tensions between the professions.

During the post WWII years, the profession of the interior designer began to flourish and started to enjoy an improved status. In the 1950s it was recognized and developed as an occupation in its own right. The Incorporated Institute of British Decorators (IIBD), founded in 1889, added the title "Interior Designers" in 1953. In 1976 it dropped the term decorator and became the British Institute of Interior Design (BIID) and in 1987 it became the Chartered Society of Designers (CSD).

The American Institute of Interior Decorators, founded in 1931, became the American Society of Interior Designers (ASID) in the 1970s. Within Asia, the ifiIDA (International Federation of Interior Designers/Architects) and the AIDIA (Asia International Design Institute Association) are both organizations that professional designers can become affiliated to.

Like many other creative areas of design such as graphics and industrial design, the role of the interior designer started to become the preserve of the expert. Subsequently magazines and books

reflected this newfound status, with even the long-established *Architectural Review* featuring "new interiors" within its pages.

Today interior design is recognized as a profession that incorporates a variety of disciplines. Interior designers will be commissioned to design retail, exhibition, work, leisure, event, branding, stage sets, health spaces, and even architecture. While the profession is still unlegislated in the UK, in Europe and the USA the title is recognized and practiced only by certified interior designers.

**Villa Savoye,
Poissy, France**
Design: Le Corbusier. This villa's bathroom is clinical, clean, and stripped of any superfluous decoration, which reflects the qualities of the building in which it is situated.

Interior design and education

Interior design is a complex process of combining the needs of the users with the qualities of the existing or given space, while ensuring that the proposal is sufficiently robust. It is essential for the designer to have a great understanding of building regulations and planning laws, an extensive knowledge of materials and finishes, a familiarity with building techniques, and an awareness of costs. The interior designer is also expected to have a working knowledge of the history of the subject and be aware of current trends.

And all of the above must be combined with the creative ability to produce interiors of merit.

The interior designer is usually educated in one of two ways: the first and most usual is to gain a validated qualification, and the second is through a period of apprenticeship. Inevitably most designers combine the two—nearly all newly qualified interior specialists begin work in design offices as assistants or juniors. The profession has its roots in the guilds and trades of upholstery and painting, and so

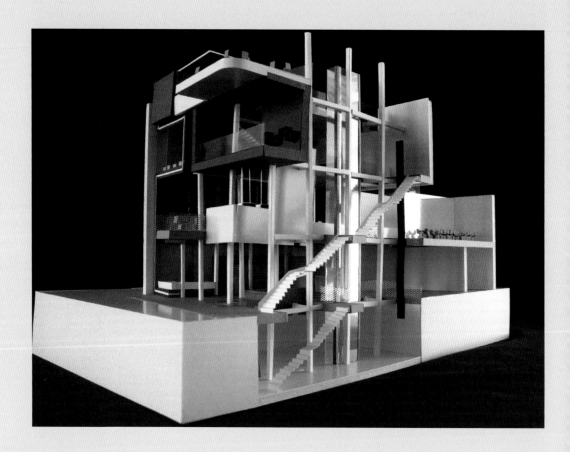

until the mainstream emergence of interior design education, most training was through apprenticeship, that is, learning through doing. Many of the notable practitioners from the early twentieth century, such as Elsie de Wolfe, were untrained; in fact, de Wolfe started her career as an actress. Designers relied instead on a good visual sense and a great deal of confidence.

The formal education of an interior designer usually begins in an art school. Many art schools were founded in the mid- to late-1800s. Institutions such as The Central School of Arts and Crafts in London, the Manchester School of Art, and the Nottingham School of Art began around this time, and followed a general Arts and Crafts curriculum along with apprenticeship programs. The Bauhaus model of arts

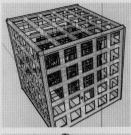
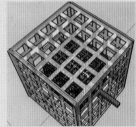

Opposite: Winebank Project, Interior Design, Manchester School of Art, UK
Design: Rachel Vallance. Modelmaking (both sketchmodels and final presentation models) is just one the tools by which the student designer learns how to express their ideas.

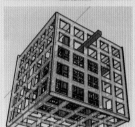

Below and right: Sketchbook, Interior Design, Manchester School of Art, UK
Design: Michaela O'Hare. Students are encouraged to research precedents and experiment with ideas. This research can be recorded in many different ways, such as drawings, models, and sketches. Three-dimensional sketches explore the formal qualities of the design.

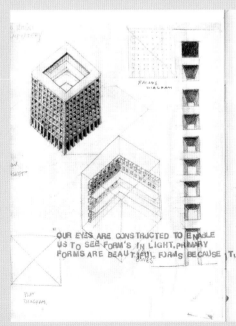

aldo rossi

education in the 1920s and 30s superseded this. The student's education began with a general introduction to all the arts (as preliminary learning or a foundation), through to the central core of architecture. This training would ensure that students experimented with many different types of design and materials, such as glass, wood, metal, weaving, painting and decorating, and so on. The Bauhaus model is still influential today.

The USA has a long and established tradition of design education. The Parsons School of Design in New York specialized in the training of interior designers as early as 1896. This was followed by the New York School of Interior Design in 1916, and much later, the Fashion Institute of Technology course in 1951. Within Asia, there are many courses in interior design and interior architecture. A number of these are affiliated to universities in the USA and the UK. This encourages the students to be aware of international contemporary design. In the UK, the education of the interior designer was formalized by the middle of the twentieth century. By 1968 five art colleges ran a diploma course in interior design and, at the instigation of Sir Hugh Casson, the Royal College of Art established the first

Processes within, and through, the site

postgraduate course. However, because still today in the UK, the education does not include a professional qualification, unlike say, architecture which is validated by both the RIBA and the ARB, interior design is still troubled by issues of amateurism: "Many architects refuse to believe that such a thing as interior design exists at all. Some place it on a par with the art of the milliner or pastry cook; others seem to regard its claims for separate consideration as a personal affront." (In-scape)

Despite international diversity and differences, the majority of these courses do follow a similar format; they encourage the student to learn through experimentation. The student is asked to design a series of theoretical interiors; that is, they are expected to propose a solution for an imaginary client, but usually in a real situation. Within this process, they are required to sketch, draw by hand and on the computer, create models, investigate materials and finishes, and have a knowledge of regulations and costs. This is generally supplemented by lecture series and building visits.

Students can now study the many different aspects of the subject, from straight interior design, interior architecture, interior decoration, history of interiors, theater design, retail design, and hotel design, to name just the most prevalent. Building reuse is also studied within schools of architecture. The large number and variety of courses across the world reflects the different aspects of interiors-related education.

The title that many professional interior designers use to refer to themselves as has been joined by interior architect and also spatial designer and environmental designer. Issues of sustainability have ensured that the design of interiors and the remodeling of existing buildings are fast becoming major sectors within the building industry, and the education of the interior designer is beginning to reflect this importance.

Printing Studio and Road Sweeper Refuge, Interior Architecture, Brighton University, UK
Design: Jo Mattsson. Students can study many different aspects of the subject and explore not just the interior but also the exterior and environmental concerns. This drawing shows the connection between inside and outside spaces.

Interior sensibility

The training and education of an interior designer is based around the understanding of the constraints and possibilities of working with an existing building. This promotes a certain kind of sensibility; that is, an acceptance of what is already on-site and a willingness to accentuate those found qualities. The designer can work with the narrative of the existing building; they can choose to emphasize particular aspects of the place. This may be as simple as acknowledging the context or aspect through the use of openings or windows, or it may be a complex uncovering of the strata of history hidden within the construction of the building.

The existing building will offer many clues to the manner in which it can be adapted. This is often unrelated to function, because of course, the same activity can occur in a number of different types of spaces. The designer will read the intrinsic qualities that are embedded within the host building, and use these as the basis for the approach to the remodeling. As architect and academic Rodolfo Machado explained in his seminal essay "Old Buildings as Palimpsest," "...in remodeling, the past takes on a value far different from that in the usual design process, where form is generated 'from scratch.'"

When remodeling an existing building, the designer will place importance upon the process of the analysis; that is, the study of the context, history, and structure of the existing building. The act of creating new uses for existing buildings, of incorporating spaces that were constructed for a particular previous purpose, provokes the designer

Halfords store, UK
Design: Ben Kelly Design. The reuse of "found" objects and elements is a particular interior sensibility. It is a strategy that is exemplified by Ben Kelly in his designs for auto parts retailer Halfords, where objects such as telegraph poles, graphic signs, and road markings are positioned in the interior to striking effect.

into accepting or editing previous patterns of existence. This reworking is sometimes often thought to be the sole territory of conservationists, who certainly can contribute to the process. However it is a much more radical and controversial spatial discipline. The act of creating interior space is a strategy that is naturally transgressive, it is an act that interprets, conforms to, or even disobeys existing orders.

This type of attitude is epitomized by the use of the "found object." Marcel Duchamp first coined the phrase when he used a series of "off-the-peg" objects such as a urinal and a bottle rack to create unique art pieces. Interior designers such as Ben Kelly, Casson Mann, and Klaus Block understand this sensibility, and approach the reuse of existing buildings with a certain attitude and response.

Cross-disciplinary concerns

The study of interiors is plagued with misunderstandings, misassumptions, conjecture, and supposition. One possible reason for this is that it is hard to identify the exact parameters of the subject. Interior design is often described as a hybrid discipline, overlapping with other spatial or object-related practices. This is partly rooted in its history and its emergence from the crafts of upholstery and scenic painting, but is also due to its connection to architecture as a space-making discipline and also the relationship that the subject has with conservation and preservation.

Architecture could generally be typified as working with new builds and starting from scratch, while interior design is characterized by working with the existing, whether that is an old building or the drawings of a structure. In this sense, architecture could be described as utopian in that it aims for longevity and timelessness, often seeking to create buildings that may stand the test of time and are produced on a greenfield site. Interiors, on the other hand, are often designed to be temporal, sometimes required to reflect the vagaries of fashion or the transitory requirements of clients who regularly require new retail spaces, offices, exhibitions, or leisure-time space.

The study of interiors obviously has a close connection with architecture, and additionally with conservation, preservation, restoration, and sustainability. Installation art and land art are also closely aligned subjects, in that they both analyze and interpret existing situations. Interior designers are expected to have

knowledge of product, industrial, exhibition, museum, and furniture design, and they are often asked to design the objects that populate their interiors. Two-dimensional design subjects, such as graphic, surface pattern, and fabric design, are also areas of interior design.

Another field of creativity is theater set design; the creation of a stage setting for a performance is akin to the design of interior space as it is usually inside, site specific, contained, and temporary. Other cross-discipline connections can be made with any practice that reuses space and objects. Some connections are more established than others. The restoration of paintings is not so readily connected with interior design although its translation or interpretation of historic material on canvas is not unlike the reuse of the fabric of an existing building. Music, and the interpretation of a score are like the reinterpretation of a building. Each practice analyzes, translates, and reuses what is already there. The study of these other disciplines is relevant to interior designers, as the particular sensibility and approach that these artists and designers may take is often similar to that taken by the designer of interiors.

The interior designer/architect will often work together with designers from other disciplines. The most obvious collaboration is with an architect, but other common relationships include those with the conservation architect, graphic designer, product designer, and lighting designer. The designer of interiors will also form relationships with engineers, including the structural, electrical, and services engineers.

The study of interiors is a cross-disciplinary activity that shares common ground with many other creative practices. This can be viewed as an invigorating endeavor, the freedom of which is liberating. The design of interiors is an activity that is not constrained by the rules and boundaries that limit so many other subjects.

Left: Kvadrat showroom, Copenhagen, Denmark
Design: Bouroullec brothers. Furniture, textiles, and lighting are dramatically combined with graphics to theatrically project the brand image of the Danish textile design company within its showroom.

Right: Sverre Fehn retrospective exhibition, Venice Biennale, Venice, Italy
Design: Sverre Fehn. The design of exhibitions is just one specialism within the spectrum of different disciplines that intersect with interior design.

Adaptation

Interior designers generally have one of two types of space to work with. The first is the existing building. The designer will thoroughly analyze this given collection of spaces before proposing a strategy for change. The second type of space is the unbuilt structure. The interior designer has to fully comprehend the intentions of the architect before embarking upon a design proposal. This may involve more than just establishing the position of the structure, openings, and materials; it can also encompass an understanding of the theoretical approach that the architect is taking. If this discussion happens early on in the design process, the architect and the interior designer can develop a mutually advantageous relationship, where the inside and the outside of the building are developed in tandem.

Adaptation, or remodeling, is the process of completely altering a building. The original use or function of the building is usually the most obvious change, and this modification will often require significant alterations. More often than not, adaptation will involve the creation of new rooms, the formation of new circulation routes, and a significant change in the relationship between particular spaces. This process is also referred to as adaptive reuse, reworking, interior architecture, and interior design.

"Alteration is more like a duet than a solo. It is about the art of response as much as it is the art of individual genius; it sets out to make a concord between the new and the existing, or even a discord. Either way, it is a proposal concerning how the designer may form a response in their new work to the host building." Fred Scott, On Altering Architecture

The reuse of an existing building to create a new interior space is a robust process and one that may involve the selective demolition and rebuilding of a site. The designer will be commissioned to not only design an interior, manage a budget, and liaise with contractors, they will also be required to make judgments on which areas of the existing building are to be retained and which are to be destroyed.

Dundee Contemporary Arts, Dundee, UK
Design: Richard Murphy Architects. The plan for this new arts center incorporates the remnants of an earlier existing warehouse and extends it to create a new building.

Therefore the reshaping of a building and its contents poses the difficult question of how to address the meaning and value of the existing built fabric. The relationship between the existing and a new adaptation is dependent upon the cultural values attributed to the existing building, by the economics of the project, and by the approach of the designer of the new addition.

Of the three, the economic factor is the easiest to establish. Adapting existing buildings is labor intensive whereas new build tends to be capital expensive; adapting buildings is energy saving whereas new build generally consumes enormous amounts of energy and resources.

The cultural value attributed to an existing building is harder to discern. This will involve

many subjective things such as its history, its importance, the quality and type of the construction, and even the affection felt by the surrounding community for the building. All of these values may be subjective and not easy to reach consensus upon, therefore the judgment of the designer plays a crucial role in adapting buildings.

In 1985 architectural historian Ignasi de Solà-Morales outlined a theoretical framework for understanding the adaptation of existing buildings. In the groundbreaking article "From Contrast to Analogy: Developments in the Concept of Architectural Intervention," he describes remodeling as a concept that is closely related to the understanding of history. Solà-Morales also understood the foolishness of establishing a too rigid formula for remodeling buildings:

"It is an enormous mistake to think that one can lay down a permanent doctrine or still less a scientific definition of architectural intervention. On the contrary, it is only by understanding in each case the conceptions of the basis of which action has been taken that it is possible to make out the different characteristics which this relationship has assumed over the course of time." The remodeling of existing buildings is a complex process that combines an understanding of what is already there with an appreciation of modern technology and design. Each project needs to be considered individually as each has a unique set of requirements and conditions. The approach that the designer takes is subject to many influences and, therefore, it is a process of reconciliation and negotiation.

Dundee Contemporary Arts, Dundee, UK
Design: Richard Murphy Architects. The reworked building is a composition of old and new elements. These are woven together to form an atmospheric space that would be impossible to create just by constructing a new building. The external realm of the street is brought into the interior to connect the city with the inside of the building. The new thoroughfare links together the internal functions of the center such as the café, movie theater, store, galleries, and reception.

Restoration, preservation, conservation

The design of interiors and the remodeling of existing buildings is a vast subject that can range from ephemeral installations that last little more than a couple of hours to the wholesale and painstaking restoration of a listed structure. The act of conservation, of preserving an original building, creates a continuity with the past. It recognizes the worth of the already built and that this can provide a link with the past that is impossible to comprehend from other sources. As architect and academic Jorge Silvetti explains in his essay "Interactive Realms," buildings can be the only records we have of certain eras: "At the risk of sounding too partisan and biased, I would say that even in historic times documents were not always available, and buildings (monuments, vernacular constructions, and public works) are themselves important texts, often providing the first and most lasting impression of a culture."

Working with an existing building inevitably requires the designer to respond to the value and condition of what is already on site. There are a number of different approaches to the problem of working with an original structure, and which approach is used will depend on the cultural worth of the building (including its listing on a national register), the approach of the client, and the condition of the structure. Conservation is a term that is used to encompass many of the different approaches, but it is possible to further categorize them.

Preservation maintains the building in the found state, whether ruinous or not. The building is made safe and any further decay prevented from occurring, but no attempt is made to return the building to its original state or to update it for modern needs. The act of preservation places value on the current condition of the building and facilitates the historical understanding of the place. For example, an historic monument that is preserved in a ruinous state.

Restoration is the process of returning the condition of the building to its original state; this often involves using materials and techniques derived from the original period of construction. This process attempts to replicate the original appearance of the building and so attempts to make it appear unaltered despite many centuries of use. For example, a church can undergo extensive repair that does not alter the form or nature of the building, but does prolong its useful life.

Renovation is the process of renewing and updating a building, for example a palace or large mansion might be adapted for twenty-first century living but not substantially changed.

Remodeling is the process of adapting the building for a new use. This could involve massive alterations to the fabric of the building and changing the function.

Sometimes two of the methods may be employed in unison. The Cathedral Museum in Lucca, Italy, is contained within a small collection of historic buildings; a thirteenth-century town house, a sixteenth-century church, and a seventeenth-century storehouse. These were carefully restored before the designer, Pietro Carlo Pellegrini, remodeled the buildings by inserting a modern walkway into and through them. This served to tie the different structures together.

Attitudes toward the conservation of existing buildings have radically altered over the last century. The Athens Charter of 1931 generally recommended that restoration work should respect the existing building, regardless of the style or period, and that any alterations or additions should be clearly differentiated from the original. It also recommended that the evidence of preservation should be made obvious. This was done with the best of intentions: to preserve history, while not confusing or compromising it, and to emphasize the importance of conservation rather than restoration. The Charter was drawn up in reaction to the then fashionable procedure of either restoring a monument to its original condition—thus removing any evidence of passing time—or the practice of "updating" the building, that is restoring or remodeling it in the contemporary style. The signatories of the Charter rejected historical pastiche and insisted upon the importance of interventions within historical areas being made in a modern architectural language.

Raven Row arts center, London, UK
Design: 6a Architects. A fire in 1972 severely damaged the interior of this Grade One listed eighteenth-century townhouse. The careful and sensitive restoration of the fabric of the building has given the interior a new lease of life.

The problem with this kind of approach is that it led to uncompromisingly modern structures being constructed, often overpowering and diminishing the original buildings. The Italian architect Carlo Scarpa was the forerunner of an alternative approach that rejected the Athens Charter and advanced a method based upon a sympathetic understanding of the existing building. Scarpa's approach was to take all the cues for the remodeling from the existing building, with a particular attention to scale, light, form, and movement, so his design strategy was part archaeology, part analysis, and part new construction.

Left: Sackler Gallery, Royal Academy of Arts, London, UK
Design: Foster+Partners. A modern glass and steel insertion has been dropped into the space between the two older buildings (Burlington House and the Main Galleries) that house the Royal Academy. The cornice of Burlington House provides the support for the Sackler Gallery.

Above: Great Court, British Museum, London, UK
Design: Foster+Partners. The courtyard of the British Museum has been enclosed by an elegant glass and steel roof. This previously exterior space has now been reclaimed and has become an integral part of the interior of the museum.

Today the gradual acceptance and respectability of the practice of conservation is based on a reaction to the perceived detrimental erosion of the city by modern architecture. The development of conservation laws—in the USA by the 1966 National Historic Preservation Act and in the UK by the Civic Amenities Act of 1967—encouraged authorities to designate conservation areas in cities and towns, and hence retain the character and identity of the urban environment.

Found objects

Within the practice of remodeling, there are many aspects and features of the existing building that can be reused. Any unusual or out-of-the-ordinary objects, found in situ, may be retained to create a unique connection with the history of the site. After all, each and every site is distinctive and exploiting these qualities allows the designer to create an interior that is irreplaceable and inimitable. This practice of reusing site-specific elements can be described as the practice of working with found objects.

Elements, objects, or surfaces that display or evoke the history and nature of an interior can add character and worth to a space. In the redesign of the Royal Court Theatre in London, the designers, Haworth

B

Royal Court Theatre, London, UK
Design: Haworth Tompkins Architects. The interior of the first floor theater foyer is stripped back, with walls and surfaces exposed to reveal the history of the site. This is counterpointed by a bright red wall finished in smooth polished plaster.

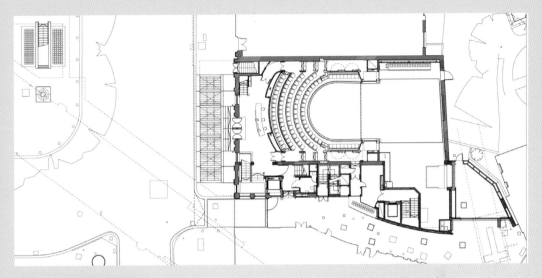

**Royal Court Theatre,
London, UK**
Design: Haworth Tompkins
Architects. Plans for the
theater redesign.

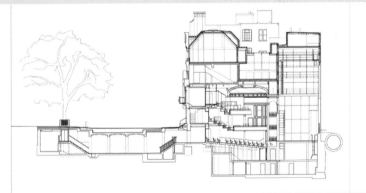

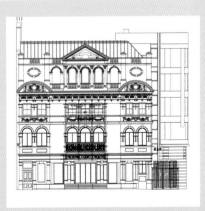

Tompkins, stripped away the accumulated deposits to reveal the bare walls of the theater foyer and auditorium. The uncovered strata of surfaces exposed previous renovations, layers of coverings and additions, and even the notes left by the original builders, which they had hastily scribbled onto the wall to remind themselves of important dimensions. These exposed surfaces formed a backdrop for the newly designed walls and objects. The raw, uncovered interior was designed to forge a strong connection to the past and to reinforce the theater's reputation for commissioning and presenting raw, uncompromising plays and productions.

As well as the use of elements and surfaces found in situ, found objects can be imported into an interior in order to create a poignant or dramatic statement. A found object may be introduced that is totally alien to the space. It could be from a different time or culture, or have a function that is completely at odds with the new use it is being installed for. Marcel Duchamp pioneered the artistic process of appropriating an object and placing it in a completely different context to which it was first intended. He used the expression "the ready-made" to describe this placement of "off-the-peg" objects, such as a urinal or a bottle rack, in an art gallery.

It is now a commonplace tactic within the late twentieth-century/early twenty-first century creative landscape to use the processes of collage, sampling, reuse, and remixing of ideas, sounds, and images in the creation of interiors. It is a typically post-modern process of design as described by Nicolas Bourriaud in his book *Postproduction Culture As Screenplay: How Art Reprograms The World*: "Artists today program more forms than they compose them; rather than transfigure a raw element (blank canvas, clay, etc.), they remix available forms and make use of data. In a universe of products for sale, pre-existing forms, signals already emitted, buildings already constructed, paths marked out by their predecessors, artists no longer consider the artistic field...a museum containing works that must be cited or surpassed as the modernist ideology of originality would have it, but so many storehouses filled with tools that should be used, stockpiles of data to manipulate and present."

Found objects can also be manipulated before they become part of a new interior. Rachel Whiteread is a highly influential artist, whose concepts and ideas have been translated into the world of design and

Embankment, Tate Modern, London, UK
Design: Rachel Whiteread. 14,000 castings of boxes were stacked in the vast Turbine Hall of the Tate Modern gallery, evoking associations of containment and storage.

Royal Court Theatre, London, UK
Design: Haworth Tompkins Architects. The uncovered layers of previous renovations and constructions forms a narrative of the life and history of the building.

architecture. She transforms found objects by making castings of them, or rather, of the space around or within them. These are not copies, they are more like simulacrums, that is, interpretations or shadowy representations.

In her early work she used everyday objects such as tables, mattresses, or baths. She made a cast from plaster, resin, or wax of the space around the object. When the object was removed, the resultant artwork reversed the order of the object/space relationship. The previously solid object had become a void and the empty space around it had become solid. Her most famous work, House, for which she won the Turner Prize in 1993, was a casting of a traditional east London terraced house. The sculpture was not actually completely solid: the interior of the building was sprayed with concrete and when this was set, the exterior walls were removed, leaving just the freestanding three-dimensional form. This extremely controversial artwork exposed the interior of the building and made it solid, thus creating a direct relationship between the inside and the outside.

Off-the-peg solutions can be used to create dramatic interiors. LOT-EK imported a cleaned and remodeled petrol tank, extracted from the back of a truck, into an apartment in New York. This was placed at a high level in the space to create a two-roomed sleeping pod in the double height room. The container was

Reactor Films studios, Santa Monica, USA
Design: Pugh + Scarpa Architects. A shipping container has been adapted to house a distinctive conference room for the film and production company.

stretched across the apartment and accessed by a newly built steel staircase. The bulkhead within the container, originally designed to stop fuel swilling dangerously about during transit, allowed for two double beds to fit exactly into the capsule. Another container was placed vertically within the space to

provide a toilet and shower room.
Found objects can be used and reused
in many ways—they can imbue a space
with atmosphere and character, create
links with the past, and generate a
dynamic juxtaposition between the old
and the new.

Sustainability

Issues of sustainability are some of the most pressing concerns for most societies at the beginning of the twenty-first century. The design, construction, and maintenance of buildings all have an enormous impact on our environment and our natural resources. Just maintaining these uses almost one third of all energy consumed worldwide. Furthermore, buildings are a major source of the pollution that causes urban air quality problems and the pollutants that contribute to climate change. Worldwide, they account for almost half of all sulfur dioxide emissions, about a quarter of nitrous oxide emissions, and 10 percent of particulate emissions, all of which damage urban air quality. Buildings produce about 35 percent of the world's carbon dioxide emissions—the chief pollutant blamed for climate change. Global warming has widespread implications and the development of sustainable ways of constructing and using buildings is one of the most important tasks facing architects and designers.

There are many initiatives designed to reduce this impact. Zero Energy Buildings are usually built with significant energy-saving features, using high-efficiency equipment, added insulation, high-efficiency windows, natural ventilation, and other techniques that drastically lower the heating and cooling loads. The Zero Energy Building is a world-wide concept; the Canadian R-2000 and the German Passivhaus (Passive House) standards have also been internationally influential. Collaborative government demonstration projects, such as the superinsulated Saskatchewan House

in Canada, and the International Energy Agency's Task 13 on energy conservation have also played their part. By 2016, all new dwellings constructed in the UK will be expected to be zero carbon. A fine example of the new generation of zero energy office buildings is the 71-story Pearl River Tower in

The Reichstag, Berlin, Germany
Design: Foster + Partners. The remodeled German Parliament building is dominated by a new dome, which evokes memories of the cupola over the original building. It acts as a viewing platform that sits atop the main debating chamber, and is also a ventilation shaft that promotes the natural movement of air.

Guangzhou, China. Built by Skidmore Owings Merrill LLP as the Guangdong Company headquarters, it uses both high energy efficiency and distributed renewable energy generation from both solar and wind.

The construction of a new building uses large amounts of energy; the procurement and manufacture of materials both uses energy and imbues these new elements with embodied energy. This is the nonrenewable energy consumed in the acquisition of raw materials, their processing, manufacturing, transportation to site, and construction.

The reuse of an existing building, to accommodate new use, is a very sustainable approach to creating new space. By adapting the existing building stock, the amount of natural resources required to construct a building is greatly reduced. The structure is already in place and quite often many of the services might already be on the site. Therefore the embodied energy in these elements can be saved through upgrade and reuse. Homes throughout the world can benefit from improved insulation, more efficient windows and doors, and updated heating systems. Remodeled buildings will, of course, never be as environmentally efficient as new buildings, but given the enormous size of the existing building stock and the importance that the already-built plays within the collective memory, the sustainable reuse of buildings is one of the most important twenty-first century considerations.

When remodeling a building, the designer has the opportunity to reinforce this sustainable approach through the selection of elements and materials that are environmentally friendly. The specification of local materials can save on transportation, and the use of natural, nontoxic materials can provide a more benign atmosphere within an existing building. Recycled materials such as reclaimed timber and steel can be incorporated into a project potentially adding character to a space.

As well as constructing a building or interior in a sustainable way, the designer can also create an interior that will be occupied in a sustainable manner. For example, rain and gray water can be recycled and high levels of insulation will cut the necessity for massive amounts of heating and cooling. Passive cooling and heating is the practice of harnessing the natural climatic conditions to the advantage of those who occupy the building. This process includes the orientation of the interior toward natural light and ventilation.

Opposite: National Assembly for Wales, Cardiff, UK
Design: Richard Rogers Partnership. Wind cowls rise above the debating chamber and pierce through the roof. This allows air movement through the space and affords maximum transparency within the interior.

Left: The Women's Library, London, UK
Design: Wright & Wright Architects. Air flows through the space creating a "stack effect" that naturally ventilates all of the interior.

The manipulation of natural light into and through an interior can save on the use of artificial light and will also provide the occupant with a connection to the landscape outside the building. Trapped solar gain can save on heating, while natural ventilation can cool a space and minimize the need for extensive air-conditioning.

Building reuse is the ultimate sustainable act, and an environmentally friendly approach to the reuse of existing buildings can lead to a particular identity for a building and the interior. The relationship between form and climate has been developed over thousands of years and is explicit within vernacular architecture. It is an area of architecture and design that is rich in precedent and ideas. Discovering and rediscovering methods of reducing energy use are one of the twenty-first century's foremost preoccupations, and the attitude taken by the designer can contribute to this debate.

Details

The details or the individual features of the interior are the elements within the space that give it its character. It is through the invention and ordering of the details that a space is given identity and thus is imbued with the power to represent a particular client, a brand, or even a culture.

Usually the details of a project are considered at a late stage during the design and arrangement of an interior. Typically, the overall strategy is developed before the actual details of the design are embarked upon. Details are usually but a small part of the whole project and yet they give the space its atmosphere. It is the detail that the visitor will first encounter within a space. Upon entering a room, it is the floor or the wall, maybe the door handle or even just the light and surface of the space that are the first things to be touched or responded to.

The designer has to consider the construction, arrangement, manipulation, organization, and juxtaposition of the individual elements in order to create a coherent and viable proposition that supports and reinforces the overall strategy for the space. The details can be described as both the individual elements that together make the whole space, and the minute design of these elements.

Details can be categorized as either off-the-peg or bespoke elements. Off-the-peg describes details that have been

Opposite: Door handle, Raven Row arts center, London, UK
Design: 6a Architects. The bespoke crafted handle is designed to fit firmly in the hand and reflect the language of the eighteenth-century building.

Right: Gate detail, IUAV, Venice, Italy
Design: Carlo Scarpa. This huge, solid gate requires a large, overscaled sliding mechanism to facilitate its opening and closing.

Below: Teatro Armani, Milan, Italy
Design: Tadao Ando. The glass desk glows enigmatically within the austere entrance space of this theater.

specified, usually from the vast array of catalogs and brochures advertising details and fittings. These are generic solutions and can be applied to a variety of design project requirements—furniture, kitchens, and even staircases and elevators are but a few examples. Off-the-peg can also relate to "found" objects and details that are used in an unusual manner and usually out of context. Bespoke is used to describe a detail that is custom-made. Bespoke details are usually built to fit the exact requirements of the project. Both off-the-peg and bespoke elements include the whole range of details from flooring to furniture; objects to fixings; light, circulation, and connecting details; and material specifications.

The fabrication of details can also be made either on- or off-site. A project that

Wonderful: Visions of the Near Future, traveling exhibition
Design: Ben Kelly Design. These exhibition objects are carefully lit to entice visitors inside. The elements are positioned to direct movement through the space.

requires a particular or unique element that might only be made by a specialist may well have to be made off-site and transported to the project. There may also be elements that can only be fabricated on the site. Any detail requiring poured concrete is a good example of a site-specific assembly.

There are a number of detailed elements that interior designers generally either create or specify:

• Vertical or horizontal planes, such as walls, floors, and ceilings are used to enclose space and make a room—the basic elements of interior design. A plane can control the visual and physical limits of a space, and can be made and finished in many different materials and colors.
• Objects such as a piece of furniture, a sculpture, a heating vent, or a large structural pod can manipulate space, movement, and visual direction. The choice of material and finish can determine the atmosphere and identity of a space.
• Natural and artificial light can control space and form. Its careful manipulation can articulate movement, illuminate objects, and change the perception of space. Whether natural or artificial, light is an essential element and the skillful articulation of it can influence the experience of a building.
• Surface is a detail that establishes a direct relationship between human contact and a building. The surface of any element, that is, the specific materials that it is made from, not only provides for the environmental and ergonomic control but also projects the identity of the building.
• Openings are crucial punctuation points within buildings. They have obvious uses, such as facilitating movement and admitting light, but they also have the less obvious function of creating views, providing orientation and direction, and, most importantly, they establish relationships between places.
• Elements that allow movement through or around a building—such as stairs, elevators, corridors, etc.—not only provide access to different areas but also serve to bind together separate or disparate spaces. Staircases, bridges, and balconies can be more than purely functional and can form sculptural and focal elements.

Whichever type of detail and its method of fabrication, the detail is the element that gives meaning and identity to a space.

Surfaces

It is the actual surface finish of an object, element or the interior itself that communicates its identity and character. The surface of an interior is often the first point of contact for the user of the space. A well-crafted surface or a thoughtful choice of material can lend meaning to an interior. The choice and manner in which surfaces are deployed is reliant on the nature of the given space, the requirements of the client, and the agenda of the designer. The response of the designer to the needs of the users can provide the opportunity to express a variety of sensibilities, ranging from the sumptuous to the austere. For example, the personality of a wall covered with distressed steel is quite different to the same wall clad with padded silk, and different again if the surface finish is made of textured rubber. The surface finish is usually not the same as the substance that a particular component is constructed from, but the visible uppermost surface. There are of course instances where these are the same thing, for example, a brick wall.

There are two methods of employing surfaces in an interior: applied and found. Applied surfaces are imported into the project and used to cover the fabric, framework, and objects within the existing building. These might range from the use of mundane "sheathing" surfaces such as plasterboard and paint, which are used to line the bare bones of a stripped back building, through to exotic rich finishes such as fine stone and expensive timbers. These complete the space and convey the narrative and atmosphere that the designer wants to project.

Found surfaces are the coverings and textures that are already in situ in an existing building. These may be interesting and can be used to expose the life story of the building. The Soviet soldiers who captured the Reichstag building in Berlin at the end of WWII scratched graffiti onto the walls. This was discovered during the remodeling of the building in the 1990s, and Foster + Partners chose to retain these texts as a narrative. The preservation and display of these slogans is a chilling reminder of the complicated history of the building.

It is the responsibility of the designer to control the identity of the interior through the manipulation of space and light and the meticulous selection of materials. Whether the surfaces are applied or found, the designer uses a palette of materials. Some designers use a very limited number with an emphasis upon clean lines and minimal detail; this can be described as a minimalist approach. John Pawson and Claudio Silvestrin employ this method of design. They often use a very small number of materials and may rely on just five or six carefully selected surfaces, which are expertly assembled and carefully crafted. John Pawson's work on the Novy Dvur Monastery in the Czech Republic, was described as Pawson as a "project of a

The Reichstag, Berlin, Germany
Design: Foster + Partners. Graffiti scratched onto the walls is left exposed as a reminder of the building's turbulent history.

lifetime." It combines the monastic, serious, and ethereal spatial requirements of the Cistercian monks with the work of a designer renowned for his careful control of light, proportion, and minimal use of materials. Perhaps surprisingly, it was the monks who contacted Pawson after seeing images of his Calvin Klein store in New York; they recognized a kindred spirit. They felt that his aesthetic could reflect their particular requirements of "no color," silence, and seclusion from the outside world. The restrained palette of materials consists of polished plaster, concrete, timber, and glass, which when combined in this thoughtful and spare manner, create an image of precision, drama, and a sense of the divine in the space.

In contrast, designers can deliberately assemble materials together in order to shock or just to revel in a riotous juxtaposition of colors and surfaces. The designer Nigel Coates is celebrated for this type of approach. The Café Bongo—part of a series of works constructed in Japan in the 1980s—was a space in which the materials, colors, and surfaces clashed wildly to create an exotic and theatrical meeting place for Tokyo's trendsetters. The café was housed in the first floor of an anonymous 1960s concrete tower block, thus allowing the designer the freedom to impose a new identity on the space. A huge airplane wing swooped through the center of the interior, dominating the space and providing for the organization of the seating and tables. The previously anonymous space was endowed with a surreal new identity. There are now many unusual materials

available for use in interiors, many of which have been adopted from unfamiliar sources and other industrial processes. These are often used in a manner for which they were never intended. Plastics, meshes, acrylics, and textile applications are now a widely accepted aspect of interior design surfaces. Doriana and Massimiliano Fuksas' design for the restaurant in the Emporio Armani store in Hong Kong is characterized by a dramatic, red fiberglass ribbon, which emerges out of the floor and becomes a bar table, and then rises before dropping to create a dining space. The journey of the ribbon continues, intersecting with the DJ stand to create a bar space, before it finally turns to become a spiral tunnel that defines the main entrance. This huge, sweeping element organizes the space and also bestows a unique identity on the interior.

It is the application of a wide variety of surface materials, some drawn from unorthodox sources, that endows a space with a particular identity. Traditional materials such as wood, plaster, wallpaper, masonry,

Opposite: Casa Batlló, Barcelona, Spain
Design: Antonio Gaudí.
The ceiling surface of the main room of the house is fashioned from plaster that swirls outward from the central light fitting.

Above: Kvadrat showroom, Stockholm, Sweden
Design: Boroullec brothers. Unusual materials can be used to cover the surfaces of interiors to create dramatic statements. This showroom for the famous architectural textiles company uses colored foam tiles as a wall covering.

Top right: Basilica San Marco, Venice, Italy
Harder materials in the form of stone tiles can be used to cover the surfaces of buildings and interiors.

Bottom right: Qiora Spa and Store, New York, USA
Design: Architecture Research Office (ARO). Long, sinuous fabric curtains are used to hide the more private and intimate areas of the spa interior.

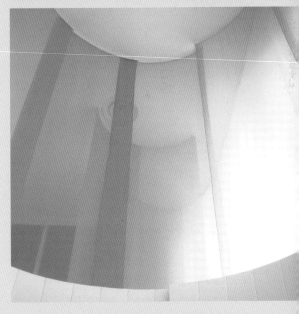

glass, and metal are often used in an orthodox manner, to create an atmosphere of constancy and respectability, while unusual or flamboyant materials can project an atmosphere of dynamic creativity. The crossover of orthodox and unusual materials can create odd yet often appropriate atmospheres.

Representation and communication

Architecture and interior design are practices that involve the detailed creation of space and structure. The scale and complexity of the construction of an interior space means that it has to be simulated and tested as thoroughly as possible before it is made; it is just too expensive and too complicated to get wrong! Because of the importance of this stage in the design process, the representation of interior space is usually made using a variety of media and techniques. This is in order to convey the look, structure, volume, form, and atmosphere of a space. There are various ways of demonstrating these things. Often it is done through drawings and models, usually at an appropriate scale to demonstrate the qualities and dimensions of the space and the way in which the space will be constructed. There are various media that can be used, ranging from industry standard digital software such as AutoCAD, Vectorworks, 3DStudio Max, formZ, and Photoshop, through to analog methods such as painting, drawing, and collaging. Sketch models aid the design process and can be quickly constructed from cardboard. Presentation models are usually constructed in a more painstaking and careful manner.

The student of interior design and interior architecture is in the strange position of only drawing the designs that they create. The end product is not the interior itself, but a representation of that interior. Unlike the graphic design student or the furniture design student, who can create the final product, the student of interior design will strive to produce a set of drawings that communicate their ideas, rather than the interior itself. It is a separate process to then translate these drawings into the three-dimensional reality of the actual interior. As Robin Evans noted in his seminal essay, "Translation from Drawing to Building:" "Recognition of the drawing's power as a medium turns out, unexpectedly, to be recognition of the drawing's distinctiveness from and unlikeness to the thing that is represented, rather than its likeness to it."

The process of representing and communicating a space is conducted in two parts. Before construction, a presentation of the design has to be made to the clients and sometimes also to the users; this is in order to show the intended volume, identity, and atmosphere. These drawings are usually flamboyant images that depict space, materials, people, and light, often in a dramatic fashion, in order to "sell" the space to clients. These images will often include perspectives, either digital or drawn. Sometimes three-dimensional models will also be used to show the volume and scale of the space.

After the presentation of these images, the designer will be commissioned and the project is started. A package of technical and construction drawings are then prepared to instruct the contractors in how to build the design. Interior design and architecture are exacting arts and cannot be constructed without fully detailed drawings. These drawings are factual and although they are sometimes beautifully drawn, they are generally for instruction only and are not in any way concerned with projecting atmosphere.

The scale of the drawings is always dependent upon what is being communicated; drawings that show how an interior is integrated with its context are usually drawn at 1:1,250 or 1:500; drawings that explain the organization of the space are at 1:200, 1:100, or 1:50; and drawings that show detail are at 1:20, 1:10, 1:5, 1:1, or even greater than real life at, say, 2:1.

Types of representation

The following are the main methods of representing and communicating plans for interiors and buildings. Often the designer will combine a selection of media in order to convey their objectives, for example, a drawing, quickly sketched over a photographic image, will communicate the qualities of a proposal in its context.

• Sketch. This is usually a quick, loose drawing which can be used to convey the ideas behind the project. It can be categorized in the following ways: conceptual, analytical, and observational. Conceptual sketches communicate the essence of the idea; analytical sketches detail the existing space; and observational drawings can be used to record aspects of a building's space, materials, and details.

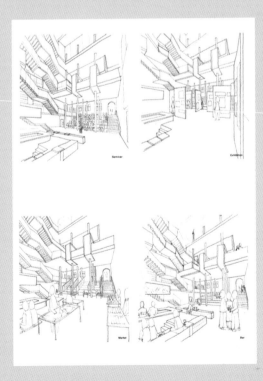

Left: Interior sketch, Fashion Institute Project, Interior Design, Manchester School of Art, UK
Design: Samantha Hart. This detailed yet loose series of sketches explore the qualities of the space.

Above: Element sketch, Interior Design, Manchester School of Art, UK
Design: Alex Johnson. The monochromatic sketch reveals the effect of light on the interior.

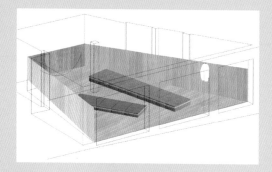

• Three-dimensional drawings. These are often used to create an impression of what it might be like to occupy a building. They are usually drawn in perspective or axonometric, and can be used to communicate the drama and intensity of an interior. They will usually depict volume, form, structure, atmosphere, materials, and light, and will often have images of people within them.

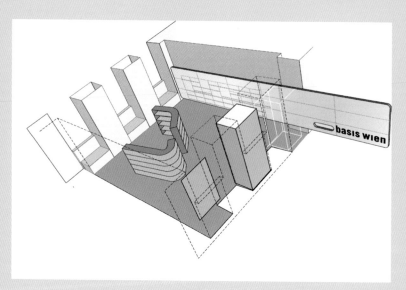

Top: oki-ni, London, UK
Design: 6a Architects. Axonometric drawing that shows the proposal for the new store interior.

Middle left: Ancoats Crematorium, Interior Design, Manchester School of Art, UK
The overexaggerated, one-point perspective drawing of the interior heightens the drama and intensity of the subject matter.

**Opposite middle right:
Basis Wien, Vienna, Austria**
Design: propellor z. The axonometric drawing of the interior of this tourist information center depicts the volume of the space and shows how the vertical plane unites the interior with the exterior.

**Opposite bottom left:
A-Poc Store, Paris, France**
This presentation drawing describes how the volume of the space is intersected by the colorful floating elements.

Below: Fashion Institute, Interior Design, Manchester School of Art, UK
Design: Samantha Hart. The card and paper model allows the viewer to imagine the relationship between the new elements and the existing building.

• Models. A model can be categorized as either sketch or presentation. A sketch model is usually constructed at speed and at scale in order to test the interrelationship of interior spaces. It is usually made from card and paper and is quite often lashed together with tape and glue. A presentation model is usually an exquisite composition that will show off a project. Computer modeling allows three-dimensional space to be drawn on a two-dimensional screen, which can then be turned and viewed at different angles.

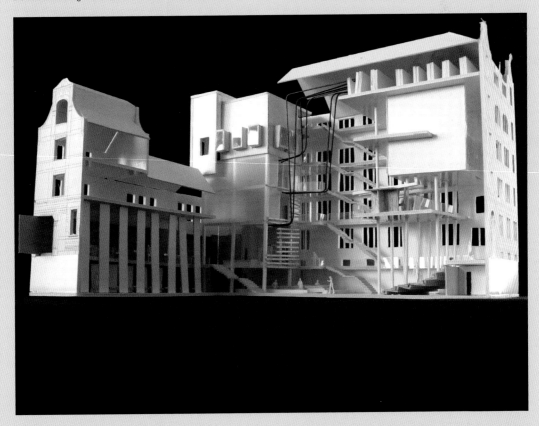

• Orthogonal drawings. Drawings such as plans, elevations, and sections communicate the facts of the scheme. The plan shows the organization of rooms and the original building. It is conceived as a slice through a building, usually at chest height, in order to reveal walls, furniture, windows, and doors. A section is a vertical slice through a building and shows the volumetric arrangement of an interior and its relationship to the existing building. The choice of where to strike a section is up to the designer, and is usually chosen to expose the most information possible in the interior. An elevation is a straight drawing of the exterior of the building.

• Construction drawings. These usually consist of plans, sections, and details that convey the information for the contractors to build the space.

• Layout and presentation. A combination of a variety of the above drawings, along with models, can be used to tell a story to a prospective client or user of the space.

Right: Layout and presentation, Interior Architecture, Brighton University, UK
This composite drawing tells the story of the project to a prospective client.

Below right: Church of Christ Scientist, Manchester, UK
Design: OMI Architects. A cross section can be used to show how embedded an interior can be within a building.

Below: Plan and Section, Interior Architecture, Brighton University, UK
Design: Jo Mattsson. These drawings show the volumetric arrangement of the interior.

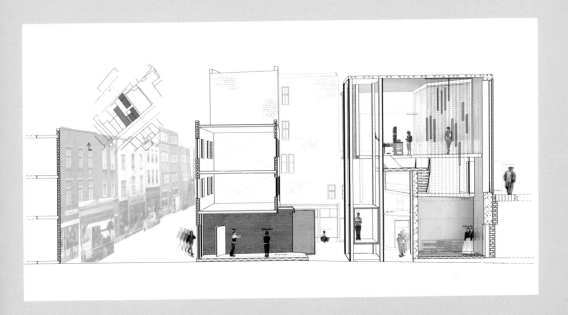

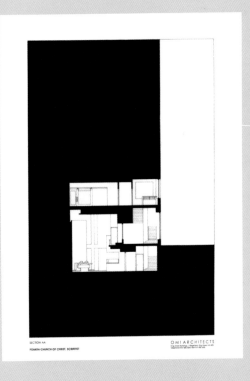

SECTION AA

FOURTH CHURCH OF CHRIST, SCIENTIST

OMI ARCHITECTS

Anatomy

The interior can be regarded as the narrative or backdrop to life. It is the manifestation of the occupier; it expresses the personality, the character, and the individuality of those who inhabit the space. The design of the interior represents the image that those who use the space want to project, whether this is responsible order or expressive creativity. Interior design incorporates many different functions and covers a multitude of different uses, each with its own particular and unique issues and concerns.

The designer will employ a particular approach to the development of the concept for the interior, whether the space is situated within an existing building or within the drawn parameters of a proposed building. This approach can usually be broken into two distinct parts—strategy and tactics—although, inevitably, there is always some overlap.

The first is the strategic or overall approach where the designer will develop a general, overarching plan for the design of the space. This will consider the interior and its relationship with things close by and far away. It will take into account such issues as structure, form, context, history, and function.

The strategic approach is often dictated by the sheer amount of integration between old and new, by the amount that the existing interacts with the proposed. It may be that the new elements of the interior take their cues from the host building; that their dimensions, materials, and form are based on the qualities of the original space so that the interior is a contemporary interpretation of the already there. This strategic approach can be described as responsive. If, however, the new and the old exist very much independently of each other, making the existing building little more than a vessel to hold the new elements and objects, then the interior is autonomous.

The taxonomy of the responsive and autonomous strategic approaches is further developed through the conceptual categories of home, work, culture, knowledge, and retail design.

The second part of the design process is the detailed development of the design, which can be described as the tactics. The manner in which materials are selected and deployed is the intimate exploration of the design of the interior. Again, this can be divided into those that respond to their context and those that do not. The autonomous and responsive sections are further classified into the individual components of the interior: light, object, plane, and surface.

Canova plaster cast gallery, Museo Gipsoteca, Possagno, Italy
Design: Carlo Scarpa. The positioning of the exquisite plaster casts within the museum space is a tactic that is designed to allow the exhibits to be appreciated while being bathed in natural light.

Strategy

When working with existing and with new space, the designer or architect will always employ a strategy for the overall design of the interior. This is a device that instructs and controls the proposal for the master plan of the space. It deals with the strategic or overall planning moves.

The design of all architecture and interiors is developed through the use of a particular strategy. This may be as simple as arranging the elements of a corporately-designed retail interior in a manner that optimizes space, encouraging the shopper to interact with the merchandise, while also projecting a particular image or brand. The strategic approach may also be a much more complex collection of contextual, ergonomic, and historical factors, all of which have combined to allow the designer to pursue a specific approach.

The strategic approach that the designer will take is often not driven by function. The approach taken to the design of the interior may be the same no matter what the activity intended for the space is. The designer will ensure that the qualities of the existing space are fully appreciated before embarking upon the proposal for the new use, and it is the response to this analysis that will drive, or provide the impetus for, the new interior.

The design of all interiors is necessarily influenced by their surroundings, and therefore by the enclosing building and its particular context. Interior designers always have to work with given space; there are always constraints that the designer has to adhere to. It is the manner in which the designer welcomes or rejects these constraints that guides the strategic approach. There are two basic methods of working with interior space: the responsive or the autonomous approach. There is inevitably often an overlap between these two systems, but it is fairly easy to distinguish between the two.

The designer can elect to fully embrace the given restrictions and limitations, and therefore propose an interior that is responsive to its contextual environment. Conversely, the designer can choose to reject the constraints and influences of the existing space and create an interior that is autonomous. That is, as far as that is possible, because, of course, there are always limitations upon size and shape dictated by the enclosing envelope. A good example of the responsive approach is a museum that has been designed to occupy a remodeled industrial building, such as a factory or warehouse. The mechanized qualities of the original building are combined with the functional needs of the new users. The Tate Modern art gallery in London, remodeled by Herzog & de Meuron in 2000, epitomizes the responsive method. The standard retail unit is typical of the autonomous interior. The only real constraints upon the design are the size and shape of the space that the store is to occupy. It is normally important for the continued development of the brand for there to be a sense of the same corporate identity throughout all the stores. Nearly all chain stores employ this autonomous approach to the design of the interior.

The following chapter is further divided into different types of functional use and discusses examples of strategic approaches to the design of these particular types of space. Home includes individual houses and apartments as well as the conceptual approach to home that the artist may take. Work encompasses the traditional office as well as more unconventional working environments. Culture embraces galleries, theaters, and community design. Knowledge incorporates libraries, museums, and educational facilities, and retail discusses the design of different types of shopping environments.

Herzog and de Meuron exhibition, Tate Modern, London, UK
Design: Herzog and de Meuron. The exhibition in the Turbine Hall was realized as a series of freestanding tables that held maquettes and prototypes of the designers' work.

Strategy: responsive interiors

When working with both new and existing buildings, the designer is always required to understand certain site-specific issues, however, the existing building can be treated as a guide, containing much of the inspiration for the redesign. The designer can respond to and embrace contextual issues such as the history, structure, or environment that the building is situated within. This responsive approach, when combined with a thorough knowledge of the functional needs of the end users, often produces extremely evocative and seductive interiors that contain a real sense of value and worth.

The designer can respond to many different aspects of the existing or new building. For example, the rhythm of the structure may induce a particular pattern to the regularity of the progression or placement of objects within the new space. The orientation of the openings or windows may encourage the designer to exploit a particular view, or demonstrate the need to provide protection from harsh solar gain. The history of the original could provide the starting point for the remodeling, as the designer and the occupiers of the space may want to explain the story of the structure. The designer can exhibit this in a manner that is both much more subtle and evocative than just straightforward printed information screens. Selective demolition is also sometimes as important as the creation of new elements; the designer may want to create some clarity within the building and to remove the accumulated additions.

Although the new interior can derive its character from the existing building, it is important to appreciate that this does not necessarily mean that it will copy or imitate its host; pastiche is often required or desirable. The designer will translate the information of the site into something new, to create an interior that contains the character and technological qualities of the twenty-first century.

The designer can take this responsive strategy regardless of the new use of the interior; it is an approach that is suitable for most functions. It is not restricted to existing buildings; a thorough knowledge of the building proposal will ensure that the designer can create an interior that is both sympathetic and appropriate to its situation.

Faversham Barn, Kent, UK
Design: Circus Architects.
The structure of the existing building has informed the placement of the new elements within the interior.

Strategy: responsive home interiors

Domestic space is often regarded as the primary focus of interior designers. This is partly due to the role of the domestic decorator in the early history of interior design and the emergence of the profession. More recently, domestic design has featured prominently in popular makeover television shows. The real role of domestic design for interiors is as a fertile ground for experimentation. There are many clues and pointers that the designer can take from the existing building that can enhance the quality of the inhabited space. The building's aspect may encourage the designer to take advantage of a specific view or light quality, or conversely, hide the view while allowing only the transit of light. The interior space can be opened up, with three-dimensional connections made within the building through the use of a mezzanine level and double-height space. The interior itself can be organized as a series of interconnected spaces or, on the other hand, it may lend itself to the removal of all the internal walls to create a free and open space.

The architect Sir John Soane extensively remodeled and connected numbers 12, 13, and 14 Lincoln's Inn Fields in London between 1792 and 1823, to create his family home. The house became a carefully reworked set of spaces that grew around its occupants and their habits. Soane was an obsessive collector and he filled the house with objects and souvenirs from his travels, including paintings by his friends Turner and Constable, casts of architectural fragments, antiquities from exotic countries, and unusual objects such as death masks and funerary urns. He even found room for the Sarcophagus of King Seti in the basement;

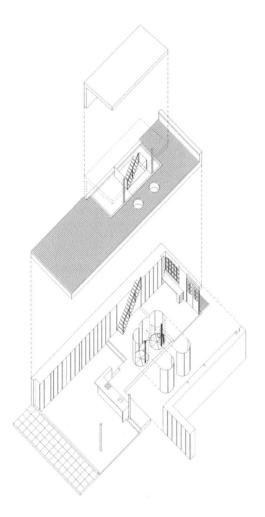

Warehouse, London, UK
Design: Simon Conder Associates. The axonometric drawing (shown on the left) describes the volume of the interior space and its relationship with the new rooftop terrace. The plans of the L-Shaped apartment are shown on the right. Note how the cylindrical bathrooms unite the different floors.

this is an enormous stone coffin, inscribed with hieroglyphs and tantalizingly displayed with the lid half open. Soane remodeled the house to contain these objects and to accommodate his family, as well as making study space for his staff and for students who regularly came to see his impressive and ever-expanding collection. The meticulous manipulation of the existing townhouse interiors allowed the house to act as a reflection of Soane's desires and aspirations. He reorientated the rooms and forged new connections in order to facilitate the life of his family. He ensured that each room caught natural light, even the basement, which was fed through a series of light funnels. This allowed him to

dramatically illuminate his collection of objects. The building and the interior still exist today in perfect harmony.

The house is required to do many things. It must offer protection against the weather, it must provide comfort, and offer an inviting place in which to reside. The home is much more than this; it contains the memories of life and the personality of those who occupy it. In a London warehouse Simon Conder Associates created a new apartment that responded to the qualities of the existing nineteenth-century warehouse. While responding to the light and volume of the shell, he set about enhancing and upgrading its facilities in order to accommodate the new domestic space. The main area was

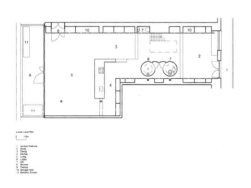

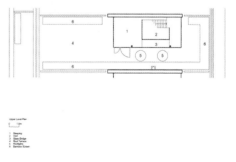

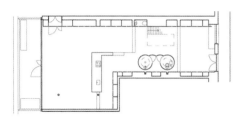

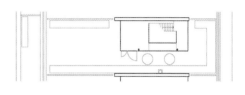

defined by three freestanding elements: a new stainless steel kitchen and two translucent glass drums: one containing a shower and the other the toilet and basin. Both drums are naturally top-lit through translucent glass roof lights. At night the drums provide the illumination of the room through artificial lighting. It is a contemporary interpretation of a domestic living space situated within an existing building; the old and the new are complemented by each other.

When remodeling a collection of terraced houses in a run-down area of Morecambe, a seaside town on the northwest coast of England, Arca Architects approached the project by tying together the disparate parts of each building with a specific material. The architects designed a series of timber elements that were inserted into the buildings. These acted to revitalize the homes and also to signal the refurbishment. Arca created an assortment of different additions, and each property received a

small selection from the collection of timber details. These ranged from relatively small elements such as dormer windows or balconies to the large-scale addition of a whole extension. The new elements were designed to be modest, yet appropriate; they are of the proper scale and the material is warm and welcoming. The use of a single dominant material served to relate each of the different additions to the individual home and also to tie the separate houses together.

Warehouse, London, UK
Design: Simon Conder
Associates. The interior is
dominated by the top-lit
translucent glass drums
that house the service areas
of the domestic space.

Strategy: responsive work interiors

The environment that is created for working in has to fulfill a number of different functions; not only does it have to provide ergonomic comfort, adequate space, and a conducive atmosphere, but it also has to represent the identity and ethos of the company. The reuse of an existing building can contribute to that brand image. An old structure, if it is converted in a sympathetic manner, can convey an atmosphere of traditional reliability, however, the designer can deliberately construct an interior that contrasts with the existing spaces. This can give the impression of a company that is progressive and dynamic, but still aware of its professional responsibilities.

The KMS Design Agency office in Munich, Germany, designed by Lynx Architects, is situated within an old factory that was previously used for the construction of trucks. Within the disused industrial building, three distinct areas were created. The largest insertion was the general open plan working space, which was placed upon a raised plinth in the center of the room. The single step up to the plinth ensures that the space detaches itself from the main fabric of the building and appears to be like a piece of freestanding furniture. It was constructed from timber, which was then covered with wool to increase the element's acoustic and insulation

**KMS Design Agency.
Munich, Germany**
Design: Lynx Architects. The cafeteria and library are both enclosed within their own environments; the library in a folded steel plane and the café is set on a concrete plinth.

capabilities. In the more intimate end of the hall, the designers placed the cafeteria and library. The cafeteria is formed from a concrete slab that is also raised from the ground by the height of a single step. A series of elegant timber benches and long, slender tables provide the informal furniture. Opposite this is the library, which is enclosed in a large channel of rusted steel that is lifted from the factory floor. The new interior responds to the formal organizational qualities of the original building and reflects the industrial character of the former use.

The responsive workspace can be designed to embrace the qualities of the existing building and the local environmental conditions to create an interior that has a unique character. Steven Holl Architects created the offices for the global investment and technology development company, D.E. Shaw, by carving a pure space from the 39th and 40th floors of a skyscraper in midtown New York. The employees have to keep pace with world markets and thus are required to accommodate the different global time zones by working shifts over the 24 hours of the day. Their workspace is designed to reflect this. The spectacular location of the office and restraints upon the budget—a large proportion of which needed to be spent on the latest digitial technology and, in case of a power cut, their own energy supply—ensured that only cheap, easily transportable materials could be used. The reception is a perfect double-height cube that filters both the spectacular view and the abundance of natural light. A simple screen wall, constructed from timber stud frame and plasterboard, surrounds it. This wall is notched and carved with a group of small windows, some of which provide views or vignettes of adjacent building façades, a number admit natural light, while others are false and are fitted with artificial lighting. At night the apertures are lit providing a calm and reflective reception space, before the workers go to their office space and carry out their duties. The interior is a clam and reflective space, responding to its extraordinary function, location, and view.

The need to expand meant that Clive Wilkinson Architects had to access the attic level of their office, which is based in a converted warehouse in London. They designed a new concrete staircase that allowed easier access to the top floor. The 13¾ foot (4.2m) wide staircase was then extruded to become the fantastically wide worktable. At almost 328 foot (100m) long, the table slides through the main space, uniting the disparate workstations. It is of an appropriate size to fit into the massive warehouse space; the sheer scale of the building would have overwhelmed anything smaller. To mitigate the hardness of the table and to offset any acoustic issues, a series of multicolored padded fabric lampshades hang in rows above the table and complete the appearance of an overscaled domestic dining table. The single element of a suitable magnitude reflects the progressive ethos of the company while tying together the different activities within the office.

Strategy: responsive culture interiors

The development of an existing building for reuse as a venue for the arts can create an unusual and remarkable interior. The creation of a new identity or atmosphere within an existing space is a process that is not the same as when creating an interior within a new building. The vagaries of the original structure will imbue the interior with a unique ambience; the reuse of existing buildings can confer identity and character on a unique or well-established organization. Because every situation is different, each existing building is distinct and individual; it is the responsibility of the designer to evaluate the precise amount of this character that can influence their new design. This analysis has to be combined with a thorough knowledge of the needs of the end users. Cultural venues such as performance spaces can be influenced by the sound, structure, and form of the host; theaters can be directed by the arrangement of the internal rooms. Therefore the reuse of

an existing building for cultural use can result in a close fit between host and new interior.

The original Young Vic theater in London, designed by Bill Howell in the 1970s, echoed the experimental nature of the company. It was conceived as a set of temporary spaces surrounding a "theater in the round." It was originally constructed to last just five years, however, a quarter of a

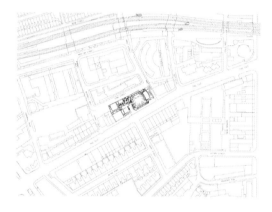

Above: The Young Vic Theatre, London, UK
Design: Haworth Tompkins Architects. Site plan of the theater. The building is ensconced in its urban environment, occupying a thin site that is bounded on all sides by housing and roads.

Left: The Young Vic Theatre, London, UK
Design: Haworth Tompkins Architects. The courtyard between the old auditorium and former butcher's shop is covered to form the main foyer.

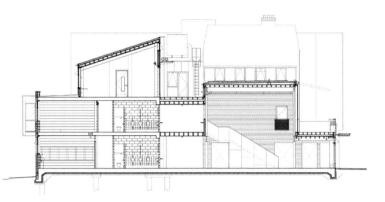

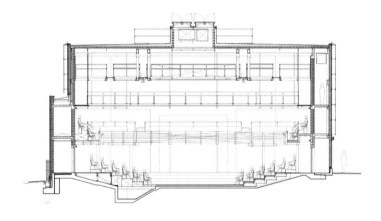

century later, the company was faced with
a rapidly expanding artistic program and the
decaying fabric of the much-loved existing
theater. In 2000, the directors of the Young
Vic commissioned Haworth Tompkins to
redesign the building. They always viewed
it as an adaptive reuse project, as their
director David Lan pointed out, "New
theaters are generally horrible." Architectural
Review, July 2007

The theater was always known for its
character and intimacy; the compact site had
enforced a close relationship between the
front and back of house. These pressures

were part of the character of the Young Vic and were to be retained. The designers did not want to construct a massive monolithic space, instead they wanted to reassemble and stitch together the disparate spaces. It is now formed into three distinct areas: the main auditorium, the rehearsal spaces, and the front of house. The front of house area consists of the an old butcher's shop that had always been on the site and is now at the center of the composition. There is no stage door at the theater and both audience and performer enter the building through the butcher shop. The auditorium was constructed from the retained, heightened temporary space, which was erected in the 1970s. The designers wrapped a new circulation around it constructed from painted cement boards with a steel mesh. This is lit from underneath, thus transforming the auditorium from day to night. The site specificity of the project is apparent; the new is very responsive to the old.

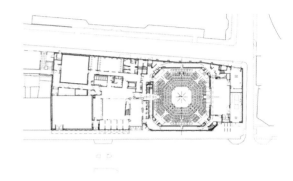

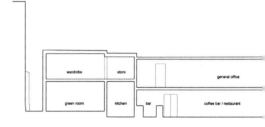

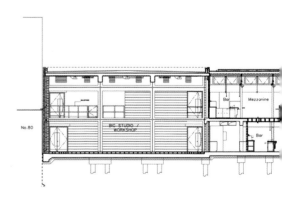

The Young Vic Theatre, London, UK
Design: Haworth Tompkins Architects. Section plans of the theater.

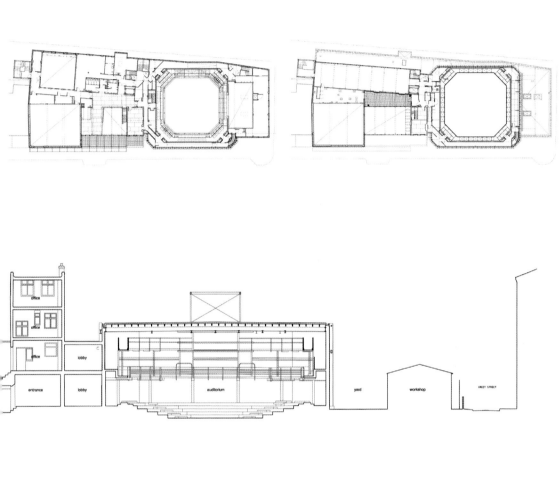

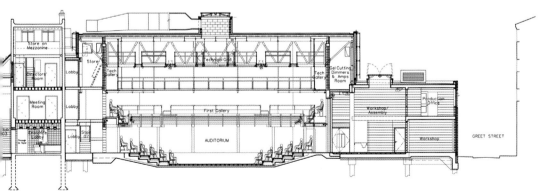

The container of an exhibition space can be used to narrate the organization and placement of a set of objects. In celebration of the bicentennial of the birth of Italian sculptor Antonio Canova, Carlo Scarpa was commissioned to expand the existing sculpture gallery at the Museo Gipsoteca Possagno, Italy. The gallery could not adequately display the sheer number of original plaster models or casts, marble works, and small sketch models that they possessed, so Scarpa created a new gallery to house this overflow. The old gallery, with its formal arrangement of objects and tall, magnificent vaulted roof, was a large, imposing space that aggrandized the plaster casts. Scarpa's new gallery alleviated the congestion of the original, while reworking its main themes of positioning, light, and scale. The new gallery consists of two interconnected elements. The first is a cubic volume, lit from above by four prism-shaped windows, and the second is a narrowing wedge, stepping down and following the shape and contours of the site. Although the language of these new areas is quite different to that of the original building, there is a direct relationship between them. Scarpa interprets the rhythm and sense of movement of the classical building and uses it as a device to control circulation through the space. He continually encourages the eye to move from one building to the next, thus introducing an aspect of promenade

Above: Canova plaster cast gallery, Museo Gipsoteca, Possagno, Italy
Design: Carlo Scarpa. Natural light pours through the roof via the corner prism lanterns and illuminates the plaster casts below.

Right: Canova plaster cast gallery, Museo Gipsoteca, Possagno, Italy
Design: Carlo Scarpa. Light slides through the wedge-shaped space of the gallery extension.

Canova plaster cast gallery, Museo Gipsoteca, Possagno, Italy
Design: Carlo Scarpa. The four prism-shaped corner windows illuminate the cubic volume of the gallery in an atmospheric manner.

into the otherwise static space and he positions the plaster casts so that instead of being focal points, they encourage the visitor to move around them.

A further cultural activity that responds very well to being placed within an existing building is the activity-specific school. The Siobhan Davies dance school is housed in an old school building in London. The original classrooms and social spaces have been reused to create new rehearsal and teaching spaces in a very modest and nonintervening manner. However, the designer, Sarah Wigglesworth, has created a new, sinuous space at the top of the building. This curved, blue timber structure adds a dramatic element to the roofline and announces the new use of the building. Dancers are encouraged to respond to the place in which they are performing; the new space is itself a piece of dancing interior architecture within the building.

Strategy: responsive knowledge interiors

It is now fairly common practice to reuse large, authentic industrial buildings to house museums and libraries, as they are generally suited to these vast spaces. It has become an imperative of Western societies to preserve their built heritage, which has meant that new and compatible uses have to be found for the buildings. The spatial needs of the nineteenth-century warehouse or manufacturing building are not dissimilar to those of the contemporary museum—large, open spaces with plenty of constant natural light. These original buildings are often situated within areas of cities that are no longer used for manufacturing, they are often too close to the city center to be accessible by large vehicles, and so their position is another reason why their reuse for places of learning and culture is both feasible and practical.

The art history department of Birkbeck College occupies a fine Grade II-listed terraced building in Gordon Square, London. Surface Architects were commissioned to transform the building and the extension into the new center for research in film and visual media. At the heart of the facility is a new 80-seat movie theater; the complex also

Left: The Women's Library, London, UK
Design: Wright & Wright Architects. The retention of these historic fragments directly connects the present with the past.

Right: The Women's Library, London, UK
Design: Wright & Wright Architects. The new freestanding block is placed directly behind the retained existing façade.

contains seminar rooms with viewing suites, academic offices, tutorial rooms, and services. The movie theater space was the initial consideration and its design became the generator for the conceptual ideas behind the project. The designers conceptually treated the interior of the building as though it was a solid block of material. They projected light through the block and then carved the light-filled spaces from it. They moved the light through the animation of the space, and then at important junctions, stopped the movement of light and removed the space again. Each "stop-frame" allowed them to open up the labyrinthine space through carving and cutting open the block of

the extension. The designers appropriately described this process as design through animation. "We think of our architecture not just in terms of photographs and drawings but in terms of YouTube and things like that… So the cinema was actually designed through animations. We didn't make the computer model in order to represent a design, we actually used animation as a means of generating the design." Richard Stott, Surface Architects. The Architect's Journal, March 2007

The normal idea of the movie theater as a "black-box" space was blown apart, to become a series of angular walls and sliced openings within the building. The journey through the interior of the space is one of clear distinctions between old and new. The interiors of the three adjoining terraces that form the front of the building facing Gordon Square have been painted gray, suggestive of the monochromatic days of black-and-white movies. As the visitor enters the extension, the interior erupts into a riot of angular, colorful walls, floors, and ceilings that spill out into a series of free-flowing spaces. This expressionistic language of the interior echoes the movies, but more pragmatically, it is an interior that removes the occupant from the everyday banality of an institutional building into a set of sequences and frames.

The Women's Library in the East End of London was founded in 1926. The peripatetic and quite disparate collection was brought together in 1977, but it wasn't until 2002 that Wright & Wright Architects designed a permanent home for the library. The designers, who have remodeled and enlarged the former public baths building, placed importance upon the retention of the

façade as a significant reminder of the old building and its associated history. The collection and study spaces are housed in a freestanding block, positioned behind the façade, but separated by a break that acts to protect the collection from direct sunlight and passively ventilates the building by encouraging the movement of cool air through the narrow gap. The new elements of the library are situated behind the façade of a building, which is a great reminder of the strength of the women's movement.

The CaixaForum in Madrid, Spain, remodeled by Herzog & de Meuron is situated in a late nineteenth-century power station. The designers have made two dramatic interventions to the building, drastic moves

Below: The Women's Library, London, UK
Design: Wright & Wright Architects. The collection and study spaces are disconnected from the façade of the building. This void facilitates environmental control, such as the movement of light and air through the building.

Right: The Women's Library, London, UK
Design: Wright & Wright Architects. Materials inside the space are suitably tough and match the robustness of the exterior environment.

which turn the structure into a responsive, open space for the appreciation of culture. The first was to extend the building vertically, so a great heavy addition was added to the structure at roof level. The second intervention contradicted this imposed heaviness; the vast mass of the existing brick building was cut open at first-floor level. This creates a vast open first-floor plane, which appears to begin at the far side of the small, open public square and continue deep into the depths of the museum. This elevation of the building and the separation of the ground floor level from the upper levels creates two "worlds," one below which is subterranean and which hosts the "black-box" spaces such as theaters, and auditoriums, and the other above, which contains the galleries, restaurants, bar, and offices. This decisive cut has liberated the building from its heaviness and neatly divided the functions along the light and dark split.

Right, top and bottom, and opposite, top left: The Caixa Forum, Madrid, Spain
Design: Herzog and de Meuron. The mass of the building floats above the ground to create a new public square which flows beneath. Derelict buildings were removed from in front of the building to create a new urban space for the display of artworks.

Opposite, top right and bottom right: The Caixa Forum, Madrid, Spain
Design: Herzog and de Meuron. The interior is accessed from a central main stair that delivers visitors into the heart of the building. The secondary staircase is a sculpted organic element within the interior.

Opposite, bottom left: The Caixa Forum, Madrid, Spain
Design: Herzog and de Meuron. The shiny and reflective qualities of the brushed steel in the bookstore contrast strongly with the decaying masonry of the exterior.

Strategy: responsive retail interiors

The design and development of the identity of the brand is an important consideration in the design of retail space. The manner in which the objects are displayed is a matter of serious importance whether these are clothes, food items, electronic goods, or perfume. The environment in which these elements are to be shown must communicate many things, because, of course, a store is selling much more than just a simple product, it is projecting a lifestyle. It therefore needs to encapsulate the identity and meaning of the designer, the brand, and the product in the way that is organised and detailed. The materials available to the interior designer are space, light, objects, and surface. Responsive retail interiors are spaces that embrace the qualities of the existing building.

The Prada store designed by OMA/Rem Koolhaas occupies the incredibly long and narrow first and basement floors of a nineteenth-century warehouse in the SoHo area of New York. These stretched spaces are

punctuated by a series of retained cast iron columns, which provide the structure for the building. To facilitate the store, the designers have inserted a remarkable floor that rolls through the length of the interior and also connects the first floor and basement together. This undulating plane links the back and the front of the store, while also acting as a display stand and shop floor. The new floor swoops through the space; it begins at sidewalk level at the façade, before dropping into the basement. Here it creates a sunken

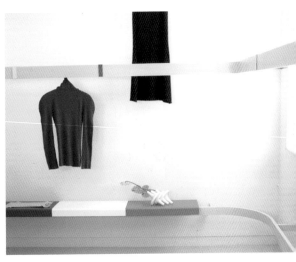

A-Poc store, Paris, France
Design: Bouroullec brothers. This store is designed to represent the process of customizing and buying "A-Piece-of-Cloth," the phrase that supplies the store's name. The interior is constructed from planes of folded Corian, and items of clothing are simply hung from the Corian strips. Bolts of fabric are displayed on benches and positioned so that they can be easily cut. Occasional flashes of colored Corian hide the junctions in the bright white interior space.

auditorium and stepped display plinth, it then folds its way back up to first-floor level and the rear of the store. The new heaving surface creates a relentless and fluid backdrop for the display of clothes. The new interior has responded to the qualities of the building by embracing and accentuating the long, thin shape of the structure with a dramatic and adventurous gesture.

An interpretive response to a particular object can inspire a designer to create a bespoke environment. The A-Poc store in Paris is one such location; designed by Ronan and Erwan Bouroullec to display the clothes of the avant-garde fashion designer, Issey Miyake. The concept for the store is a bespoke clothing service, as the customer participates in the creative process of the design of their garment, creating individual items of clothing from basic patterns. The Bouroullec brothers responded to the unusual qualities of the process and the product by using an unusual material: Corian. This is a moldable, weldable plastic that can appear to be both fluid and rigid. The Corian is used in bent and curved strips, which flow through and around the space. The interior is bounded by a series of strips of brightly colored Corian, and

connected to these are the folded stands. These are used in a number of different ways depending on the needs and circumstance: as a cutting table, a display stand, or a checkout counter. Using Corian, the interior designers have interpreted the methods of the fashion designer to create a space that is somewhere between an exclusive boutique and a factory.

Usually retail spaces are transitory and designed to last as long as they are considered to be fashionable, yet they can still respond to the vagaries of the environment into which they are placed. The Alexander McQueen store in New York treats the first floor of the existing building as a solid block of ice from which the new interior has been carved. The store is located in the meatpacking district of downtown Manhattan, where exclusive restaurants and retail spaces rub shoulders with meat-processing outlets and huge refrigeration warehouses. The McQueen store responds to this context with a clean, sharp, and sculptured interior of glacial beauty. The interior reads as though it is constructed from a series of carved ice sculptures, some hanging from the ceiling and some growing from the floor. The deep

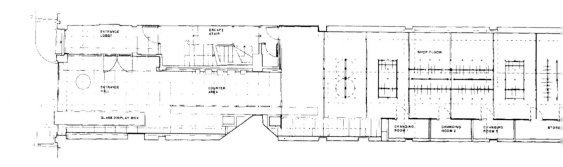

Left: Alexander McQueen store, London, UK
Design: Pentragram. The interior is designed to appear as if it is carved from a solid block of snow or ice. The junctions between the horizontal and vertical surfaces are deliberately curved to accentuate the cave-like quality of the store.

Below: Alexander McQueen store, London, UK
Design: Pentragram. It was very important that lighting and other services did not protrude through the smooth surfaces of the walls and ceiling. The lights were integrated into the display fittings and so do not interrupt the continuous flow of the elements within the space.

freezer theme is extended deep into the store; the checkout counters and display spaces appear to be hewn from the carved surrounds. Brightly lit niches are sculpted into the walls to fully illuminate the expensive shoes, bags, and garments on display. The cool ice-blue terrazzo floor accentuates the icy interior. The space is a comment upon and an interpretation of the surrounding area.

Left: Alexander McQueen store, London, UK
Design: Pentragram. The plan of the London store shows how the design concept was transferred from the New York flagshop store. The interior is long and narrow, and the designers have exaggerated this through the use of the sculptural elements that protrude into the space.

Strategy: autonomous interiors

The concept for the interior is often created away from the site or building. The new interior is independent of its enclosing shell; it is an autonomous, self-determining series of elements and spaces. The original building may be considered as an envelope into which the new interior can be placed, exerting very little, if any, influence upon it. This creation of a new interior can be regarded as a self-governing process that is constrained only by the boundary of the established spatial volume.

Although the autonomous interior may lack any meaningful connection to the particular qualities of the host building, it can still contain a characterful atmosphere and identity. The individual elements of the interior may respond to each other, forming a collection or series of connected parts, which together create an impression or specific identity.

Exhibition design is often an autonomous process; it is important for the artist or designer to convey a precise and unambiguous message, which is not diluted or confused by the building. The individual elements of the exhibition are consistent with each other; they are part of a family of related objects or display units. This is especially true of traveling exhibitions, where the constituent parts have to be sufficiently independent and adaptable to be accommodated in a variety of different environments.

Retail design is another typical example of the autonomous interior. The designer will create a brand image and from this a collection of elements that are capable of being translated into a number of different environments. The consumer expects to buy into a particular identity, they know what to expect from the image that is projected by the design of the retail unit, as much as from the items that are for sale.

The autonomous approach is suitable for most types of accommodation. It is not the precise function of the interior that drives this strategy, but it is the establishment of relationship or not between the new and the old that guides this method of design.

Mandarina Duck store, Paris, France
Design: Droog. The exclusive products are displayed on a series of freestanding elements that are placed in an autonomous manner within the interior.

Strategy: autonomous home interiors

The concept of home is something that has always been at the forefront of architecture and interior design. The manner in which the family lives is continually evolving, from the communal atmosphere of the medieval grand hall to the insular and repetitive qualities of the English terraced house. Changes in work patterns and family expectations have meant that at the beginning of the twenty-first century there is a move toward open-plan living, with the kitchen once again acquiring a position at the heart of the household. Domestic space is often completely independent of the building that it occupies. Bright and gleaming kitchens occupy buildings that are 200 years old, state-of-the-art technology inhabits adapted brick warehouses, and the need for individuality means that the interior of every home within a street is different.

The designer George Ranalli was commissioned to design a small apartment in a tiny space in a converted furniture warehouse in New York. He placed a compact, freestanding piece of furniture inside the main room. This concentrated element contained all the basic functions of the living space. The sleeping, dining, and working areas were combined into the piece of furniture, maximizing the amount of free space, both horizontally and vertically, within the tiny apartment for relaxing. Bookcases were accommodated into a set of steps that led up to the elevated bed level, that in turn sheltered a small dining table and seating. The elegant, autonomous object was positioned off-center, so that the kitchen could occupy the smaller space next to the door, while the larger, naturally-lit area was used for lounging in. Home condensed into a petite element in a tiny space with no wastage.

The interior of the home can sometimes contrast starkly with the qualities of the building that it occupies. Objects placed within the interior that have unusual qualities or meanings can imbue the house with a unique identity. The Morton Duplex in Manhattan was designed to accommodate the home for two people in a fourth floor space of a transformed former parking lot. The designers, LOT-EK, are renowned for incorporating found industrial objects, such as shipping containers, truck parts, and kitchen sinks, into their projects. The Morton Duplex is the remarkable installation of two petrol truck containers imported into the otherwise empty space. One container is installed horizontally across the apartment, the other is placed vertically on its end at the back of the space. The insides of all aluminium containers are separated by a bulkhead, which is needed to stabilize the liquid during transportation. These correspond to human proportions and form natural partitions in the vessels, thus allowing the horizontal container to be split into two bedrooms while the vertical container holds a toilet and shower. The autonomous installation is a sculptural conceptual statement that was designed to afford maximum contrast within the space of the apartment.

Sometimes the place that we call home can be reduced to its bare essentials. The autonomous house can be created from just the essential elements that are required to perform the basic functions of a dwelling. In the White Cube gallery on the campus of the University of Massachusetts, the architect and artist Allan Wexler was invited to create a living space that distilled the essence of modern living. He proposed a series of movable crates. The essential functions of the house were stripped down and organized as a series of slideable boxes on wheels that moved in and out of the main gallery. Each of the three crates that slid into the central space contained an element of essential living equipment: there were the kitchen, the sleeping, and the working crates. Each could be pulled into the main space when required and then pushed out when finished with. Crate House was a piece of installation art that proposed alternatives to the acquisitive manner of modern living.

Crate House, University of Massachusetts, USA
Design: Allan Wexler. Here, the house is reduced to its bare essentials. Each unit contains all that is necessary for human comfort. The crates can be pulled into the central space when required.

Strategy: autonomous work interiors

Working takes up a large percentage of our daily lives and it is important that the work environment is both effective and adequate. It must provide for the physical needs of the workers, it needs to be efficient in the way it allows its occupants to work, it needs to offer comfort, and provide a healthy environment. The workplace also needs to ensure that it offers emotional support, in that it needs to be a place that enhances or unites the community of employees. The character of the building and the interior is often required to represent the nature of the company, in that it conveys a message about the ideals and aspirations of the business and symbolizes its identity or brand. Hamburg's Chamber of Commerce building was constructed in 1841. It is a neoclassical building with a grand, colonnaded entrance

Chamber of Commerce, Hamburg, Germany
Design: Behnisch Architekten. The new structure is conceived as a series of stacked boxes sitting autonomously within the interior of the old building.

facing the town square. It was constructed to project confidence and engender respect, because the Chamber was a central player in the prosperous port's global affluence. Yet, due to subsequent changes in the city's fortunes, combined with the departure of the stock exchange from one of its halls, the owners of the building realized they had to rework the interior to attract new business and clients. Behnisch Architekten redesigned the interior in 2006. A new autonomous installation was placed in one of the three grand halls. The new structure takes the form of a pile of stacked boxes, which rise up six levels into the high ceiling of the hall. Each floor contains a variety of functions. On the first floor is a business startup "incubator" space, designed to entice and support new companies. The

Above: Chamber of Commerce, Hamburg, Germany
Design: Behnisch Architekten. The incubator space lightly touches the existing building.

Top and above: Chamber of Commerce, Hamburg, Germany
Design: Behnisch Architekten. The contemporary insertion contrasts dramatically with the old building; the volume of the hall is so vast that it dwarfs the new structure.

second and third floors contain offices, meeting rooms, and conference spaces for the new startup companies. The fourth and fifth floors contain an exhibition space, filled with pieces taken from the Chamber's extensive collection, alongside which is a set of flexible meeting rooms which can be transformed to more gallery space or a room for presentations. The upper floors contain a restaurant for members and visitors, and the seventh floor has a club

Chamber of Commerce, Hamburg, Germany
Design: Behnisch Architekten. The modernist language of the new workspaces is a dramatic statement within the Classical banking hall. The level of the top floor club coincides with the arched windows of the original building, offering the visitor great views across the city. Three-dimensional spatial relationships are created within the bar and restaurant. The designers deliberately left a space between the old and new, which acts to define them both.

Chamber of Commerce, Hamburg, Germany
Design: Behnisch Architekten. The designers have used an evocative technique with which to represent the difference between old and new on these atmospheric sections: photographs of the existing building contrast with line and tone drawings of the insertion.

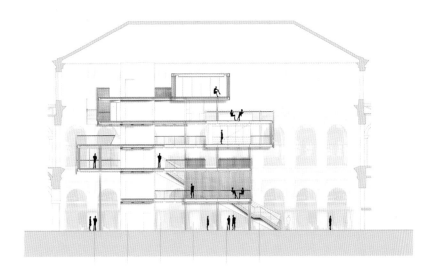

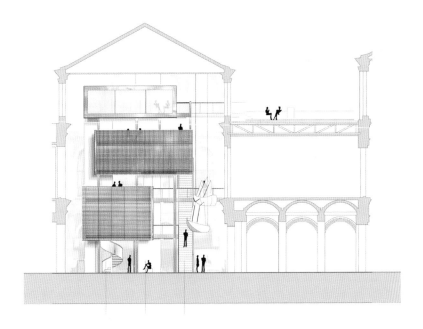

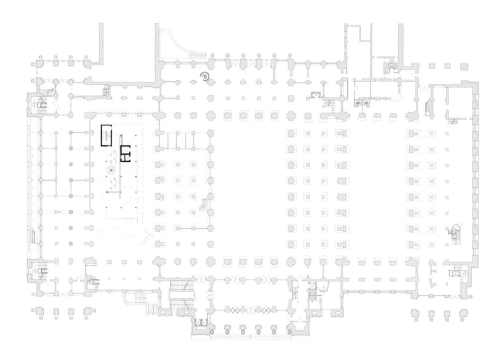

with a bar and lounge, resplendent with elegant chandeliers and old masters' paintings. The architects have created an independent structure that acts to revitalize and add a contemporary appeal to an aging building.

Left: Chamber of Commerce, Hamburg, Germany
Design: Behnisch Architekten. The strong visual connections throughout the space are made within the bar.

Top: Chamber of Commerce, Hamburg, Germany
Design: Behnisch Architekten. The plan of the building. The new element sits in the left-hand courtyard.

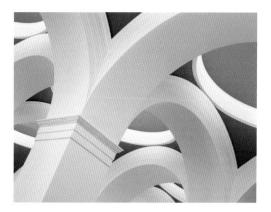

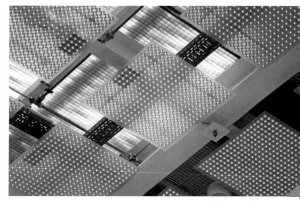

Above: Chamber of Commerce, Hamburg, Germany
Design: Behnisch Architekten. The stepped skirting of the original building.

Top right: Chamber of Commerce, Hamburg, Germany
Design: Behnisch Architekten. The vaults of the existing building.

Above and right: Chamber of Commerce, Hamburg, Germany
Design: Behnisch Architekten. Details of the soffit and its innovative L.E.D. lighting system.

Left: Chamber of Commerce, Hamburg, Germany
Design: Behnisch Architekten. The sumptuous private dining room.

When Lehrer Architects in Los Angeles decided to move offices, they chose to rework a 50-year-old warehouse in Silverlake, California. They not only wanted the space to function as a working office and to embody their values, but it was also designed to demonstrate their particular work process to prospective clients. The large, open plan space was stripped out and painted white, and the southern wall of the shed was glazed to allow an abundance of natural light to be admitted and provide a view to the new garden. The floor reinforces the organization of the building with massive painted white-and-gray stripes.

The workspace itself can adhere to this pattern when necessary, but has sufficient flexibility to be arranged in a more autonomous manner. The long desks, which were constructed from white painted solid core doors, can be arranged in a way that is most suitable for the task, rather than being permanently fixed.

Below left: Lehrer Architects, Los Angeles, USA
Design: Lehrer Architects. The rigorous order of the office is visible through the large windows of the façade.

Above and below right: Lehrer Architects, Los Angeles, USA
Design: The large open plan space allows views through the interior into the landscaped garden beyond. The desks allow the size of the workforce to shrink or grow depending on the number of projects requiring attention.

As well as creating a space in which to work and embody identity, an autonomous approach can be used to create a dramatic statement of intent. On the rooftop of a building in a discreet side street in Vienna, Austria, a dramatic new rooftop addition can just be seen peeking over the gutter. This lawyers' office by Coop Himmelb(l)au architects is a dramatic glass and steel rooftop extension that has drastically altered the Viennese skyline. The new structure has a distinct birdlike quality, and when viewed from the inside, it is a spectacular and theatrical event that represents the progressive attitude of the company.

Autonomous workspaces can unite their employees in a manner that expresses the values of the company and shared common principles. The new offices of Mother, a London-based advertising agency, are distinguished by a huge table that has the capacity for 200 people to work at. Since Mother was initially established, all of the staff have worked around a simple table. As the company grew, so did the table. The table has become the defining element of the agency.

Mother, London, UK
Design: Clive Wilkinson Architects. The huge concrete work table provides the central focus of the space.

Strategy: autonomous culture interiors

Cultural buildings and interiors often have very definite needs. These can be environmental, structural, ergonomic, or aesthetic. The designer has to completely understand the implications of these factors and incorporate them into the new design for the cultural institution. For example, performance spaces need to be able to accommodate the theater stage plus backstage areas as well as the auditorium and front of house spaces. The intricate needs of all of these will need to be analyzed and understood, as well as the precise manner of their interaction. Whether the cultural interior is within a new building or part of a redevelopment, the designer needs a thorough knowledge of the mechanisms and procedures of the organization.

The Royal Exchange Theatre in Manchester, UK, was designed to occupy a small part of the cavernous main hall of the Royal Exchange Building. Trading ceased in 1968 and the building lay derelict for a number of years, before housing a temporary theater. In 1976 Levitt Bernstein Architects installed a dramatic self-contained theater building in the grand hall. The new element epitomized the progressive optimism of the space age: the theater is reminiscent of a recently-landed spacecraft. The elegant, exposed structure is firmly attached to the enormous columns of the original building. The layers of steel and glass cladding wrap a unique in-the-round theater space, which is entered from eight different positions within the hall. The theater is famed as much for its perfect views of the stage as for the audience's proximity to the action. This is a well

thought out, autonomous object situated within a magnificent neoclassical interior.

An autonomous object that is carefully placed within an existing space can facilitate new activities within the place, while also permitting the original functions to continue. This gives each activity a degree of independence, but also invites an aesthetic contrast within the building. The more secular age of the twenty-first century has led to many church buildings having to adapt to survive. Religious and secular activities quite often now occur side-by-side within the same buildings. In London, St Paul's Church in Bow has been remodeled to accommodate a new autonomous element. This two-story

St Paul's Church, London, UK
Design: Matthew Lloyd Architects. The simple timber cladding of the new element contrasts with the highly decorated ceiling of the church.

**Above left and right:
St Paul's Church,
London, UK**
Design: Matthew Lloyd
Architects. The new object
is squeezed into the church
interior. This autonomous
object is animated by the
natural light that pours in
through the windows of the
old building.

Left: St Paul's Church, London, UK
Design: Matthew Lloyd Architects. The y-shaped columns lift the object clear of the congregation.

Below: St Paul's Church, London, UK
Design: Matthew Lloyd Architects. The new element is compact, thus leaving the majority of the space for religious use.

structure was placed within the nave of the church to house an exhibition space, community rooms, and a gym. The timber clad object stands freely above the old pews and is supported by four Y-shaped steel columns. It separates the front and back of the church, the secular activities occurring at the rear, while allowing worship to continue around the original altar.

Right: St Paul's Church, London, UK
Design: Matthew Lloyd Architects. The church organ has been left in-situ and offers a stark comparison to the robust steel and timber freestanding addition.

Exhibition design is a practice that is often autonomous; the artist may create a piece that is part of a series, or has a completely different frame of reference to that of its eventual end position. Often the artist is unconcerned as to where the art piece is displayed, although of course, many artists create works that are completely site specific. The artist may be stimulated by a particular event or by the pursuit of a specific ambience. Students from the Continuity in Architecture unit at the Manchester School of Architecture and from the Recycled Architecture Unit at the Universitat Politècnica de Catalunya in Barcelona completed a joint project that attempted to understand and react to the conditions that existed within a particular area of Manchester. The approach that they took was to construct a shelter from cardboard boxes. This was a comment about rubbish, waste, and squander. The structure was intended to resemble a small shelter,

although it was constructed from degradable material. It was not site specific and the concept was easily transferable, as indeed it was.

Above and left:
Interventions installation,
Manchester School of
Architecure, UK
The cardboard structure is a statement about the wasteful practices of the twenty-first century.

Strategy: autonomous knowledge interiors

The exhibition and transfer of knowledge is often an autonomous act. The message that the interior needs to convey is sometimes, by necessity, self-contained. It needs to communicate a specific subject, to be imbued with the qualities of that topic or theme. The building then becomes merely the container or vessel in which the elements of the interior are held. These interior elements will make reference to each other and to the subject, with often little regard for the enclosing building.

The Natural History Museum in Paris was renovated and reopened in the 1980s as one of President Mitterrand's hugely ambitious and successful Grand Projects. The existing building is an imposing space lined with cast iron columns that support three floors of side gallery spaces that rise to the glass roof. The designers, Chemetov, Huidobro, and Allio have reordered the museum's collection of zoological specimens to create a new gallery that is as much about sheer spectacle as it is about knowledge. The theory of evolution determines the character, selection, grouping, and positioning of the objects. The main exhibition space is a large hall on the first floor. On its upper side, on a plane of simulated land, is a cavalcade of animals, marching through the gallery. The great bull elephant is leading, followed by the giraffes, who are next to the zebras, and so on. Underneath this floor is the sea. The designers gathered together shoals of fish that are displayed against sheets of planar glass tipped with blue light. This subterranean level appears to float free from the edges of the existing building and the

gap is where the whalebones hang in space, as though floating between land and sea. Sea lions, walruses, and polar bears occupy large sheets of sandblasted glass. The upper galleries encircling the main hall are home to exhibits of climbing animals such as monkeys, and higher up are the birds. Perhaps the most poignant exhibition is that of the extinct or near extinct animals, which are displayed in an almost completely dark side gallery. Each animal is faintly picked out by a single spotlight illustrating its fading chances of survival. The exhibition of this dramatic and emotional collection is organized through its connection with the natural world, rather than being ordered by the qualities of the host building.

Right: The Gallery of Evolution, French National Natural History Museum, Paris, France
Design: Chemetov & Huidobro, René Allio. The first floor of the museum features land-based animals; the floor is cut away to reveal the creatures of the sea below.

Below: The Gallery of Evolution, French National Natural History Museum, Paris, France
Design: Chemetov & Huidobro, René Allio. The line of stuffed animals stretches across the first floor.

Left: The Gallery of Evolution, French National Natural History Museum, Paris, France
Design: Chemetov & Huidobro, René Allio. The animals are positioned in order to extract the maximum theatrical effect.

The reuse of a space that is listed or which is precious can often lead to interventions that are both carefully considered and have no detrimental impact upon the host space. In 2007 Office dA were commissioned to design the new Rhode Island School of Design library within the glorious main hall of a bank built in 1917. The building was designed by York and Sawyer and is listed on the national register of historic places. The main hall is 197 feet (60m) long and 115 feet (35m) wide and is topped by an elaborately coffered barrel-vaulted ceiling. Office dA were commissioned to squeeze in not just the 90,000 books already owned by the library, but also seating for 250 people; storage for 400 periodic titles; and a variety of different study, administrative, and multimedia spaces.

The restricted budget and the sheer amount of program that was needed to be fitted in to the space was compounded by the fact that the library had to be built and ready in just nine months. The designers also wanted to ensure that the proportions and height of the grand hall were not interrupted. These factors led the designers to create two prefabricated autonomous "pavilions" in the main hall, one for study and a second for the administration of the library. This pavilion controls and monitors the movement of people and books through the library. It is constructed entirely from MDF, and is simply bolted together to create an enclosure that feels light and fresh.

Supporting elements such as furniture and bookshelves are freestanding within the hall. The elaborate nature of the existing building led the designers to place autonomous elements in the space. Their prefabricated nature not only sets them at odds with the historical context, but also implies that they could be dismantled at any time.

"We wanted to maintain the scale of the banking hall...so we decided to install two objects as if they were informal elements in an ancient ruin." Monica Ponce de Leon, Office dA.

Architectural Record, June 2007

Left: Rhode Island School of Design library, Rhode Island, USA
Design: Office dA. The main freestanding "pavilion" is placed centrally within the grand hall and allows scholars to sit and study.

Right: Rhode Island School of Design library, Rhode Island, USA
Design: Office dA. The elegant historic interior is left untouched by the new addition.

Strategy: autonomous retail interiors

Interior spaces that specifically sell clothing and accessories are created to project a distinct identity. This may be to stay ahead of the prevailing fashion or possibly communicate some other sort of image. They are designed to convey a particular lifestyle, which, in the twenty-first century is fast evolving. The design of these spaces is important; the consumption of the retail elements confers identity upon the consumer and the brand that is being sold, therefore the language of the space must accommodate the identity of the consumer and of the brand. The autonomy of the design is a vital consideration; the interior should be designed to be able to be quickly changed, updated, or even rebranded when necessary.

Mandarina Duck is an Italian luggage company that also sells clothes. Droog Design were commissioned to create the transferable overall concept for the company and also for its flagship store in Paris. The location is one of the most fashionable streets in Paris, situated within the heart of the designer showroom area. Mandarina Duck adopted an unusual strategy to develop their identity. Droog were commissioned to create a concept that could be interpreted in a variety of ways, and then, in order to differentiate the stores across the world, local designers would be approached to translate the idea in each particular situation. The solution was to install within each store an identical series of freestanding objects called "cocoons." These elements were intended to display the products for sale, but the exact method of doing so depended upon the individual designer. The cocoons were described as: circle, tunnel, wall, curtain, and enclosure. The cocoons display the Mandarina Duck products, but the articles for sale are actually concealed within them. It was intended that the process of discovery ensured that the products become precious, as the beauty of each item was examined. Within the flagship Paris store, a curving curtain of thin, translucent plastic lines directed customers through the store, a 11½ foot (3.5m) diameter metal doughnut hid clothing within it, a stack of internally-lit plastic pallets held handbags, a wall of metal pins grasped luggage, another wall of elastic bands suspended purses, and a circle of long, white fiberglass canes defined the changing rooms. This autonomous group of elements had a relationship with each other but not necessarily with the building or space that they are placed in, although they often are displayed in a manner that provides the building with maximum impact.

Mandarina Duck store, Paris, France
Design: Droog. The store interior is populated with a series of "cocoons" that display the products in an unusual and inventive way.

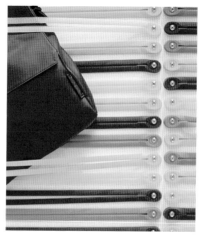

The installation of a collection of objects can ensure that the host building becomes little more then a stage for their performance. Sometimes a witty, playful idea can enliven the interior space and it is this juxtaposition that communicates the identity of a particular retail space on to the visitor. The Viktor & Rolf store in Milan, Italy, is unforgettable due to its unusual quality—it is upside down. Almost every detail of this surreal, neoclassical interior has been fitted the wrong way up. It contains parquet flooring on the ceiling and chandeliers sprouting from the floor. An inverted colonnade frames the display cases, and a grand arch becomes an upholstered

seat with elegant cushions placed daintily upon it. It is only the clothing and, of course, the customer that is upright. The upended interior, this stage-set space, creates a new perspective on the work of the fashion designers, communicating their particularly light-hearted, but classical brand.

Fashion retailing can embody a strong ethos and vision. In order to stay ahead of the competitors, new and innovative ways of capturing a visitor's imagination, attention, and most of all custom, are important. The term guerilla store has recently emerged in fashion circles to describe a quick-hit retail space that has maximum impact. Dover Street Market, the Comme des Garçons London flagship store, is a six-story building that was designed with a chaotic, market-like atmosphere. Rei Kawakubo devised the concept: "…a kind of market where various creators from various fields gather together and encounter each other in an ongoing atmosphere of beautiful chaos: the mixing up and coming together of different kindred souls who all share a strong personal vision."

Kawakubo enlisted different designers for each floor of the building, creating a mass of clashing and contrasting ideas. All ideas can be easily changed and the autonomous nature of the activity and the space provides the main excitement of the interior.

Viktor & Rolf store, Milan, Italy
Design: SZI Design and Buro Tettero. The playful inverted interior of the store confuses visitors and suspends belief, as chairs are fixed to the ceiling while chandeliers rise from the floor. Neoclassical arches become cushioned seats and parquet flooring becomes a ceiling surface inside the rooms.

Tactics

The details of the design proposal, that is, the intimate detailed design of the individual elements can be described as the tactics. This included the materials, surface finishes, shape, form, and nature of the components and constituents of the interior.

It is these elements or tactics that become a detailed expression of the character of the interior space. They express use, function, occupation, atmosphere, personality, and they differentiate one place from another. They define quality,

characterize the space, and provide individual character. For example, the designer can strategically place a particular element in a specific position, but this object could be detailed in a number of different ways and constructed from a variety of different materials. Thus the designer has the opportunity to create the image or ambience of an object from a number of different possibilities. A staircase is traditionally constructed from timber, but it is quite conceivable for it to be built from

stone, steel, or glass. However, the designer may want to project a contemporary image and could deliberately design the structure from plastic or rubber and install interactive lighting or computer screens.

These tactics support the strategic approach. The designer will make use of the analysis and understanding that informed the strategy to guide the detailed design. The tactical employment of materials and elements can also support the designer's particular approach. The tactics can be responsive to the container or building that the interior is situated within. They can act in a receptive manner and accept or embrace the qualities and character of the host building. Equally, they may act in an autonomous manner, referring only to themselves and the others in the particular group or series.

This chapter is divided into two sections: tactical details that are responsive and those that could be referred to as autonomous. Each of these sections is further divided, in a conceptual or abstract manner, so that the many detailed possibilities of an interior design are discussed. These subdivisions are light, object, plane, and surface. Light can be natural or artificial. Of course, without light, the forms and nature of a particular place cannot be appreciated, but the designer can manipulate the manner in which light is used. It can be subtly controlled to add contrast, drama, and atmosphere to an interior. A purposely-placed object can direct movement, control space, or act as a focal point. A plane can be positioned vertically or horizontally, and at its most simple is a floor, ceiling, or wall, but the designer has the opportunity to express much more with this versatile element. Surface is the material finish of an object or space, and as such can express the very character of an interior.

The tactics form an extensive, expressive, and significant design vocabulary, and it is the meaningful manipulation of these that imbues the interior with its qualities and character.

Samples, Ben Kelly Design
The language and aesthetic of interior design is frequently expressed in the use of various selected and found materials and finishes, often referred to as "samples."

Tactics: responsive interiors

The responsive interior will often act in a sympathetic manner to its immediate surroundings; this most importantly and obviously includes the host building, but also takes account of other conditions and circumstances. The architectural and interior designer frequently has to be aware of contextual issues that may have an effect on the quality of the space; these include the climate and the availability of materials, the structure and form of the building, and the physical nature of the surrounding environment. Other issues that can influence the interior design may include historical events, the previous use, and any earlier changes made to the building.

Investigations into the vernacular will offer many responsive clues to the design of the

interior. The particular context in which a specific type of architecture has evolved creates buildings and interiors that are completely suited to their situation. Many of the issues are concerned with environmental control; the passive cooling or warming of space, the admittance of sufficient natural light, the control and obstruction of the prevailing wind, and of course protection from the rain. The detailed manner in which the building responds to these issues have evolved over many hundreds of years, and an exact or meticulous twenty-first century interpretation of the detailed design can imbue an interior with a sense of tradition and worth.

The design of the building and its interior can also respond to historical events. The architect or designer may choose to celebrate or draw attention to certain occurrences or incidents. This may be a cathartic act of renewal and purification, but it could also be a commemoration or tribute to a particular incident. The detailed manner of this response can be made with the use of the appropriate combination of materials and forms.

The interior designer has always to be aware of the structural limitations of the host building. If the proposed intervention is heavy and/or unstable, then consideration has to be given to the support of the new elements or objects. The manner in which the new and old are integrated also needs detailed consideration; whether they touch, are butted up against each other, overlap, or a deliberate and precise gap is left will contribute to the atmosphere of the new interior.

A comprehensive and meticulous study of the existing can inform the tactical deployment of the detailed design. The manner in which the individual elements within the interior are manipulated will imbue a space with character. Through the use of materials and forms and detailed design, in a subtle or ostentatious manner, the designer can connect the interior with its situation.

Pantheon, Rome, Italy
Design: Unknown (commonly attributed to Marcus Agrippa). The open oculus allows light and rain to pour into the building throughout the year.

Tactics for responsive interiors: light

Interior spaces can be organized through the use of both natural and artificial light. The careful manipulation of both can lead to spectacular results.

The Dulwich Picture Gallery in London, designed by Sir John Soane in 1817, is widely regarded as one of the best exemplars of the use of natural light to exhibit paintings. Soane was commissioned to create a series of rooms to display a collection of art bequeathed to Dulwich College by the King of Poland. As well as designing a succession of top-lit rooms for the artworks, Soane was also required to create a mausoleum for the two patrons of the museum, Sir Francis Bourgeois and Noël Desenfans. Their remains, along with those of Desenfans' wife, are interred in a vestibule at the center of the west wing of the museum. The mausoleum is a tall, octagonal-shaped room with a roof light. This lantern is glazed with amber-colored glass and as the light pours through it into the room, the mausoleum is filled with a melancholic amber glow. From this atmospheric space, the visitor then enters the main gallery, which is filled with pure, natural light that falls through the roof and illuminates the paintings. This sequence of distinctive spaces, that is this journey from the tranquil mausoleum to the optimistic gallery, is almost analogous with the reaffirmation of life.

Artificial light can be used to make the most dramatic of effects within an interior space. For example, lighting within theater and set design is incredibly important and is a powerful tool for exposing and developing narrative and effect. The use of varying amounts of lighting equipment can create all walls, rooms, corridors, and spaces. The installation artist James Turrell uses artificial light with which to create and manipulate space; he regards it as an artistic medium, very much as a painter would think of paint. In his projects such as Wall Works or Veils, powerful projectors and light sources were positioned behind partitions and screens in order to project lines of light and shadow. The lines were so powerful that they appeared to be solid and so the block of light seemed to float free from the walls that it was projected onto.

When used together natural and artificial light can be a potent force. In the Kvadrat showroom in London both light and color have been used to maximum effect. Kvadrat are a Danish company famous for supplying many of the world's greatest interiors with textiles and textile-related products. Their new showroom is in Shoreditch in London, and has been designed by the graphic designer and art director Peter Saville and architect David Adjaye. The showroom is situated in a large, Victorian factory. It operates on two levels, with offices on the first floor and the

Dulwich Picture Gallery, London, UK
Design: Sir John Soane.
The series of enfilade top-lit galleries offer a bright contrast to the dark and melancholy mausoleum.

Left: Kvadrat showroom, London, UK
Design: Peter Saville and David Adjaye. The new staircase is dramatically lit and entices visitors into the basement of the showroom.

showroom in the basement, although much of the first floor was removed, thus connecting both of these levels within the building. The basement is accessed by a large dramatic staircase, which becomes the focal point within the interior. Tall panels of glazing, which are colored and designed to reflect the natural light as it pours in through the building's windows, enclose the timber stair. The colors were inspired by Peter Saville's record cover

designs for the band New Order, in particular the single "Blue Monday." At night the dramatic expression of the stair is reversed; it appears to glow from within, as recessed artificial lights illuminate the treads on the stairs. Both natural and artificial light are used to maximum effect in order to enliven the usually mundane process of moving between the floors in a building and encourage visitors to access the basement store.

Left: Kvadrat showroom, London, UK
Design: Peter Saville and David Adjaye. The stair dramatically exploits the three-dimensional quality of the space. Within the basement the visitor can access samples of Kvadrat fabrics, which are displayed in special pull-out "cells."

Left: Kvadrat showroom, London, UK
Design: Peter Saville and David Adjaye. The long elegant timber tables reinforce the orthogonal qualities of the space.

Below: Kvadrat showroom, London, UK
Design: Peter Saville and David Adjaye. The large windows allow natural light into the cavernous space.

Tactics for responsive interiors: objects

Whether small or large, an object can be used to define an interior. It can, for example, act as a focal point within a space or encourage movement through different rooms. Its qualities can be responsive in that it can be designed and constructed to exactly fit within the confines of the interior.

Sites that have unusual or extraordinary characteristics can lead the designer to create equally remarkable interiors. In Madrid, Spain, the new Architectural Documentation Center was formed within the long arcade of a disused building and a disused tunnel of the underground platform below it. The tunnel had extreme dimensions: 351 feet (107m) in length and yet only 28 feet (8.5m) in width. In stark contrast, the upper level arcade was a grand neoclassical building originally built as an exhibition hall. To link

Architectural Documentation Center, Madrid, Spain
Design: Aparicio + Fernández-Elorza. The interior is situated within a disused tunnel; the designers have embraced the linear quality of the original space and accentuated it through the use of robust and uncompromising surfaces.

the two spaces the designers, Aparicio +
Fernández-Elorza, opened up the floor of
the arcade and placed the lecture theater
in the now double-height basement tunnel.
However, this dramatic intervention
structurally compromised the integrity of the
arcade, and in order to rectify this, the new
subterranean lecture theater was necessarily
designed as a huge 19½ inch (500mm) thick,
U-shaped concrete channel that braced the
exposed sidewalls. This top-lit room serves
as both lecture theater and conference
space. It also allows for all of the services to
be hidden behind its walls and acts as the
main circulation between the upper and
lower levels. The new object responds to the
original structure, the long, thin tunnel. It is
built to fit and is an appropriate response to
the uncompromising context.

**Architectural
Documentation Center,
Madrid, Spain**
Design: Aparicio +
Fernández-Elorza. The
transition point between the
ground-level entrance and
the basement-level platform
of the original building is an
extraordinary, double-height
space that has been reused
as the lecture theater. A
structural U-shaped floating
floor accommodates all the
functional needs.

Exclusive retail objects, such as exquisite designer furniture, need a suitable backdrop to communicate the quality of the piece, which by association also conveys the ethos of the company. In 2000 the relatively unknown designer Lindy Roy was commissioned to design the new Vitra headquarters in an old warehouse in the meatpacking district of New York. The showroom not only needed to display the range of contemporary furniture and famous design classics, but also had to accommodate Vitra's offices and headquarters. The organization of the three-story premises was simple, with the showroom on the first floor, the gallery in the basement, and the headquarters housed within the upper floors. All floors are linked by a display element known playfully as "the tongue," a gray rubber folding element that swoops down through a slot in the stairs and displays the furniture over all three levels. The first floor to basement stair is placed along the tongue, thus allowing the three-dimensional display objects to be viewed from all sides.

**Left: Vitra showroom,
New York, USA**
Design: Lindy Roy. The heavy
and oppressive nature of the
basement is exploited to
display the furniture in a
dramatic manner.

**Below left and right: Vitra
showroom, New York, USA**
Design: Lindy Roy. The gray
rubber folded "tongue" slides
down through a void at the
front of the store.

Tactics for responsive interiors: plane

The introduction of a wall, screen, floor, or ceiling into an interior can be a process that allows a designer to unite the various elements of the interior. A plane, whether vertical or horizontal, can be used to respond to the eccentricities of the host building and facilitate new functions within the space.

A new wall can be used to unify a space and tie together its various elements.

Within the Museum Quarter in Vienna, Austria, the designers propeller z created a long, horizontal plane that connects the interior with the exterior of the Basis Wien, an information center situated within a remodelled eighteenth-century stable block. The wall begins outside and appears to be suspended over the stone staircase. The Basis Wien logo is clearly inscribed into the floating plane. It slides through the doorway and into the main room, which is quite simple and unadorned apart from the elegantly coffered ceiling. As the plane enters the room it becomes thicker and deeper in order to accept the shelves and drawers that hold information and books about the artists in the museum. It also houses audio-visual equipment alongside the leaflets and postcards. It is raised from the ground and does not touch the ceiling, and is also lit

Above: Banq restaurant, Boston, USA
Design: Office dA. The striated timber ceiling flows across the interior creating a fluid atmosphere within the space.

Left: Basis Wien, Vienna, Austria
Design: propellor z. The vertical plane slides from within the information center and elegantly announces itself in the courtyard.

above and below, thus giving the impression that it is floating. This dynamic element is constructed from a steel frame and clad in sheets of brushed aluminum, which contrasts with the rough, decayed surfaces of the grand room it inhabits.

A plane can be a useful device with which to respond to the vagaries of an existing building and accommodate very particular functional requirements. Office dA remodeled the main halls of an old bank building in Boston to house Banq, a new restaurant. The restaurant required enormous amounts of new services to satisfy the strict local building codes.

As well as creating the right identity and ambience for dining, part of Office dA's brief was to hide these services. The designers have installed an undulating ceiling plane that disguises the services and creates a particular identity for the space. The new plane has been modeled using Rhino software, a sophisticated 3-D package that allowed the designers to wrap the ceiling around both the services and the structure of the building. It also enabled the complex element to be constructed. This economic solution has resulted in a series of undulating fins of AplePly, which are slotted into a set of crossbeams and then clipped into place. The services, which are painted matte black, can be glimpsed through the gaps in the fins and if necessary accessed for maintenance. Lights are slotted between the fins. Bamboo flooring and freestanding tables finish the effect while striated bamboo wall screens provide the backdrop for banquette seating at the edges of the room.

In the foyer of the Norman Foster-designed Commerzbank in Frankfurt, Germany, a new dining and exhibition space has been created by Alfredo Arribas. Entitled "The Plaza," the space has been designed to accommodate a number of functions, including as a cultural space and a café, which can serve up to 1,200 staff a day. "Der Wurm," as its title suggests, is a long, undulating curved timber floor that wriggles through the space and is organized to correspond with the fan-shaped foyer space. It is a floor plane that rises up at various points to create bench seating. Hidden beneath each bench is an elegant steel and glass table that can be slid out of the floor at busy times, to extend the seating capacity by up to another 100 people. The undulating plane creates a playful and colorful addition to the stark, sober surrounds of the banking headquarters.

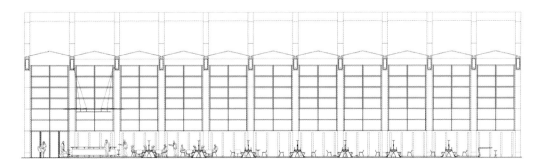

**Above: The Plaza,
Frankfurt, Germany**
Design: Alfredo Arribas.
This section shows the long,
undulating form of the
new element within the
cavernous space.

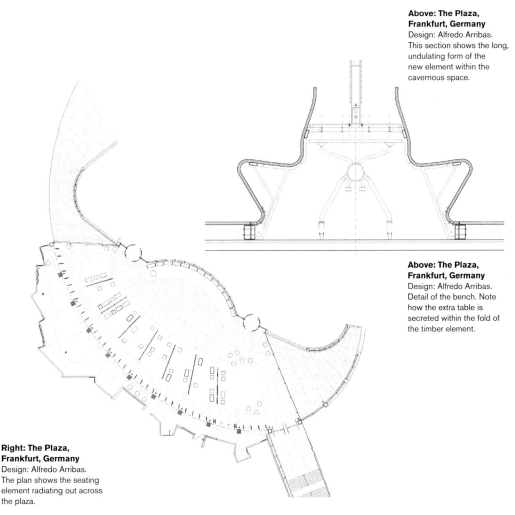

**Above: The Plaza,
Frankfurt, Germany**
Design: Alfredo Arribas.
Detail of the bench. Note
how the extra table is
secreted within the fold of
the timber element.

**Right: The Plaza,
Frankfurt, Germany**
Design: Alfredo Arribas.
The plan shows the seating
element radiating out across
the plaza.

Tactics for responsive interiors: surface

The application of a particular material endows an interior with a unique identity. It is the top surface of all the elements of the interior that the user has direct contact with. Therefore the manipulation of surface is a critical decision for designers. The responsive surface can be simply organized into two categories: existing and applied. Existing is as implied, the retained surface of the original building, and applied is any new surface specified by the designer.

Social spaces, particularly those where people meet to eat and drink, require the careful selection of materials and surfaces. Appropriate materials are needed to both create a suitable atmosphere for socializing and also to ensure the environment is

hygienic. McInnes Usher McKnight Architects (MUMA) designed the new café at the Victoria and Albert Museum in London in 2006. It incorporates the period rooms of the museum into a new modern redesign. The existing spaces of the museum included the highly regarded nineteenth-century refreshment rooms designed by William Morris and Philip Webb, James Gamble, and Edward Poynter. Each of these spaces is highly ornate and covered in elaborately decorative surfaces. MUMA worked with these found surfaces and restored them back to their former glory. The tiled surfaces of the main room originally designed by James Gamble were restored

Victoria and Albert Museum café, London, UK
Design: McInnes Usher McKnight Architects (MUMA)
The highly ornate decorated surfaces of the existing space act as a backdrop to the contemporary installations. The journey from the old to the new is heightened by the contrast in surface detail.

back to their colorful and intricate splendor. In contrast to these ornate rooms, the new café space is elegantly decorated using simple materials, such as oak and mild steel. The new and the old complement one another, each accentuating the particular qualities of the other.

The surface of an element is the component of a space or object that receives the most human contact. The manner in which materials are used creates atmosphere and mood. A limited palette of materials can give a space a distinct and individual quality. The work of designers such as Claudio Silvestrin and John Pawson is often referred to as minimalist because they use just a few well-chosen surface materials. The Johan menswear store in Graz, Austria, is characterized by this simple aesthetic. The store is based in two arches set into a sloping street in the center of the city. Silvestrin used three main materials: gray-green polished plaster for the walls, the changing rooms, and display spaces; limed oak for the long display shelf running through the center of the space; and polished concrete for the floor. The elements are put together in a sparse and fastidious manner, with 3mm shadow gaps used carefully to separate the display elements and the floor. The raw and unusual setting is emphasized by the spare and refined installation.

Color and surface are closely related and are important considerations in the design of interiors. While materials can be used in their natural state to give identity to an interior, the painting or covering of surfaces is also a useful and often economical method of creating a distinctive environment. The necessity for clean, hygienic surfaces within surgeries and other health-related situations is very particular and also well regulated. As well as hygienic considerations, the identity and atmosphere of the interior needs to be inspiring and friendly in order to calm any nervous patients.

Nobody likes visiting the dentist to have their teeth fixed, and it's an even more daunting prospect for children. Graft Lab was commissioned to design a children's dentist in Berlin, Germany. The client had seen the designer's work for bars and restaurants and decided that it would be interesting to transfer some of those design ideas to the interior of his practice. The surgery is located in a three-story, nineteenth-century building, which incorporates a split-level entrance. Large double-height windows on the façade let enormous amounts of natural light into the building. The designers decided to link all three levels with a curved plastered wall.

Above: Johan store, Graz, Austria
Design: Claudio Silvestrin. Three polished plaster enclosures form the changing rooms within the store.

Left: Johan store, Graz, Austria
Design: Claudio Silvestrin. Polished plaster, limed oak, and polished concrete are the three different surface finishes used throughout the interior. They are meticulously assembled and detailed.

**Left: Kinderdentist,
Berlin, Germany**
Design: Graft Lab Architects.
The curved, painted timber
wall links all three levels of the
building and unifies all of the
functions of the surgery.

This was constructed from a simple timber
frame construction and painted in various
shades of tropical ocean blue. The vertical
wave wall slides through the space and
links the basement waiting space with the
upper level treatment rooms. The blue is
designed to calm patients and help them
imagine relaxing by the sea. Openings
within the wall allow light into the rooms
behind it and views out of the space. It also
helps to break the unrelenting quality of
the colorful surface. This is a new element
that links the different spaces within the
building and invigorates the interior.

Tactics: autonomous interiors

The detailed manner in which an interior is expressed can be separate and disconnected from the exterior. The quality of the interior space can reference only itself, that is, be independent of outside influence and have little or no relationship with the host building. Traditionally interiors were self-contained, self-referential spaces. They were designed to function in a particular manner that was self-serving and expedient. Indeed, until the advance of modernism the interior of a building could quite viably exist independently from the exterior.

Castles and other stately buildings had great thick walls that acted to mediate between the shape of the room and its container. The use of niches, cupboards, and other concealed spaces allowed the room to develop an identity that was not controlled by the form of the building. Architecture and interior design were different and independent activities.

Modernism and the pursuit of transparency have blurred the difference between inside and outside. The need for the activities that occur within a building to be reflected on the exterior, combined with massive amounts of glazing that have made the boundary wall indistinct, has meant that the truly autonomous interior is a thing of the past, and more promisingly, the future.

The eighteenth-century interior has many fine autonomous qualities, many of which act to divorce the interior from the exterior. Tactics such as thick, book-lined walls allowed the room to assume the appropriate shape for its task. Cupboards and niches permitted a round or octagonal

Livraria Lello bookstore, Porto, Portugal
Design: Xavier Esteves. An elaborate, sculptural staircase dominates the breathtaking Gothic interior of this bookstore.

shape to exist within square-shaped walls, and a succession of differently contoured spaces could be formed within a regularly shaped building.

The difference between inside and outside is also exploited in more contemporary

architecture and interiors. Retail, exhibition, and furniture design are the most obvious examples. The shape, nature, and character of the individual elements are dependent upon the needs of the users and the agenda of the artist or designer. Also, the move toward decorated façades and the use of double-skin cladding within contemporary architecture, has once again put distance between the interior and the exterior, and allowed the designer to celebrate the autonomous quality of inside space.

Tactics for autonomous interiors: light

Natural and artificial light can transform a space in a profound and dramatic manner. Within a building, light can alter the user's perception of space and add excitement to the sequential promenade through a building.

Exhibition design relies enormously upon lighting effects to display objects. The Groninger Museum in the Netherlands is a curious building that was conceived as four connected pavilions which were created by four different designers. The buildings sit on the edge of a canal and appear to float upon the water. Philippe Starck designed the pavilion for the applied arts section of the museum. This part of the display was housed in a huge circular steel drum, which was set into the canal with no windows and therefore no

Applied Arts exhibition, Groninger Museum, Groningen, the Netherlands
Design: Philippe Starck. Diaphonous floating curtain screens surround the hard, engineered display cases. The artificially-lit room is highly atmospheric and theatrical.

natural light. The gallery consists of a series of tough, highly-engineered glass and steel cases that house the delicate porcelain and ceramic exhibits. The circular drum wall of the exhibition space surrounds these display cases. The main room is then organized by a series of diaphanous curtains that hang from the ceiling and which surround a series of freestanding cases. Each heavily plated curtain is top-lit with a thin curved fluorescent tube, washing the fabric with a gentle and atmospheric light. The visitor to the gallery becomes a shadow as they pass around the curtained "rooms" in the space; voices and figures are fleeting as they pass from one exhibit to another in the gracefully atmospheric room.

Natural light can be used to shape and alter a room, and can also be used to illustrate a junction between new and old within a space. The Kolumba Art Museum of the Archdiocese of Cologne, Germany, designed by Peter Zumthor, is a building that meshes an old ruined church with a new gallery for religious art. The first floor of the building is a composite of what remains of the original church with the new walls placed directly upon these ruins. Natural light filters into this spiritual space through groups of tiny openings in the perforated brick wall. This provides sufficient low-level light to adequately illuminate the preserved remains, while lending an ethereal quality to the interior space.

As well as animating interior spaces, light can also be used as a symbolic material with which to impart a message. The lower floors

The Kolumba Art Museum, Cologne, Germany
Design: Peter Zumthor. Light is used to articulate the junction between the contemporary architecture and the ruins.

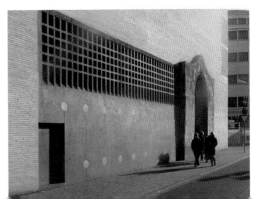

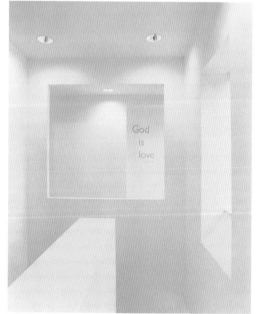

Far left: Church of Christ the Scientist, Manchester, UK
Design: OMI Architects.
Concealed lighting glows evocatively within the double-height worship space.

Left, above and below: Church of Christ the Scientist, Manchester, UK
Design: OMI Architects.
A simple statement placed within the alcove of the circulation space.

Right: Church of Christ the Scientist, Manchester, UK
Design: OMI Architects.
The structure of the existing building is artificially lit, exposing spaces beyond the main worship area.

of a 1960s office block in Manchester, UK, have been remodeled by OMI Architects to create a church. The worship space is contained within a double-height interior that has been carved deep into the plan, while the circulation, reception, store, and offices are placed at the edges of the building on the first and second floors. The

designers effectively scraped out a large void for the chapel. Natural light is filtered through the circulation areas and into the chapel, providing the space with a slightly ethereal quality, while artificial lights, concealed behind the exposed structure, imply spaces beyond those that are immediately experienced.

Tactics for autonomous interiors: objects

The placement of an independent object within an existing building can provoke some interesting reflections upon the nature of the element itself. The contrast between the new object and the site in which it is placed is an opportunity for the designer to juxtapose the unusual with the usual and thus create the potential for an intense reading of the autonomous element.

Exhibition design involves the creation of what is usually a neutral space, in which a series of objects can be organized around a coherent theme. Exhibitions can range from being permanent and site-specific, to temporary. A temporary exhibition will often treat the building as just a container for the exhibits, a space that the new exhibition occupies. Therefore the form and shape of the site merely provides a backdrop for the show. The eleventh Venice Architectural Biennale, held in 2008, was entitled Out There: Architecture Beyond Building. Its curator, Aaron Betsky, challenged exhibitors to offer critical alternatives to the man-made environment as a response to the title of the exhibition. Within the depths of the Cordiere exhibition space (the vast former rope-making factory of the Arsenale) was the installation for the Chilean Pavilion, "I Was Here." The designers' response to the theme of the exhibition was to fashion a huge number of crude timber plinths, fabricated from crates and packing cases, each set upon four spindly timber legs that raised each plinth to eye level. Placed on top of each closely packed together plinth, was a small model, which represented Chile's diverse architectural landscape. These models ranged from small churches and

"I Was Here," Chilean Pavilion, Venice Architectural Biennale, Venice, Italy.
Design: Aravenna, Castillo, Cruz, Del Sol, Frohn, Rojas, Irrarrazavel, Klotz, Mozo, Puga, Radic. The sparse and charming exhibit consisted of a series of freestanding elevated crates, each displaying a small porcelain maquette of a building from Chile. Each exhibit was lit by a naked lightbulb.

thatched houses through to modernist office blocks and contemporary cultural buildings. Each exhibit was illuminated by a bare light bulb that hung from a wire above the panorama of buildings.

Within retail design, an autonomous object can generate a statement about the products for sale. The designer can create an object that will become the focus of the space, thus allowing the product to become associated with that object. If the space that is to be inhabited is well known or even

renowned, then the designer needs to react to these qualities. On the first floor of 30 St Mary Axe in London, a building affectionately known as the Gherkin, Jamie Fobert Architects were commissioned to install a cake shop. The designers did not emulate the language of the surrounds, but instead created an installation that obviously fits into the space but is not joined to it. The main autonomous element of the space is a new mezzanine that hangs in the double-height room. The upper level contains the kitchen and private areas of the store and floats above the shop and café area. This huge element acts to mediate between the prominence of the building and the tiny cupcakes. Full-height windows throw enormous amounts of natural light into the store, illuminating the mezzanine and the counter and allowing the presentation of the cakes to take place in crisp, natural light.

Freestanding furniture is probably the most autonomous element within an interior. It can be moved around, placed against walls, or stand in the middle of a room. It can be cheap and easily fixed together in flat-pack form, or it might be expensive, classed as a designer classic, such as a Mies van der Rohe Barcelona chair. Whatever form it takes and however it is placed in a room, it can communicate enormous amounts of information about the room, its function, the decisions of the designer and the status and desires of its user.

Freestanding furniture for use in an office is usually fairly nondescript, with the design dictated by ergonomic and economic considerations plus the need to satisfy basic functions. The Bourellec brothers were approached by Vitra to develop a range of modern office furniture, objects that would encourage creativity, interactivity, and lateral thinking among the users in any office environment. They started with the traditional idea of a large family table around which everybody could gather, the concept

Konditor & Cook cake store, London, UK.
Design: Jamie Fobert Architects. The cavernous space of the cake store is just a small room at ground level within the enormous building.

Joyn furniture, Vitra
Design: Bouroullec brothers.
The large tables unite their
users through the shared
worksurfaces.

being that although everyone may be doing
something different, they bond simply by
being together. The table allows workspaces
to be joined together and also separated by
small dividers when necessary. Wires and
cables, phone leads, and lights are all
carefully dispensed with in the new wireless
office and the Joyn Table allows everyone to
work together and to communicate as a
unified force.

Tactics for autonomous interiors: plane

The vertical plane is an essential tactic of a theater or stage set—the "theater flat" acts as the backdrop to a performance, it can be painted, illuminated or act as a shield. A stage set is designed to narrate a particular show and is subject to the skills and whim of the set designer. Set design focuses upon the spectacular or on the meaning of a play, and because its sole function is to interpret and then communicate an idea, it can be refreshingly free of the functional requirements that most interiors are subject to. The Teatro Olimpico in Vicenza, Italy, is one of the oldest surviving Renaissance theaters in the world. Designed by Andrea Palladio and Vincenzo Scamozzi in the 1580s, it houses a stage set that is permanent yet autonomous. The stage set contains seven street scenes that recede away from the viewer with exaggerated perspective. To create this, visual trickery is employed: a gently sloping floor and walls retreat from the façade or proscenium. The exterior of a city has been reproduced in the interior space of the theater, a streetscape that reflects the machinations of the city back to its inhabitants. This is all presented behind the proscenium screen, which is a fixed ornate classical plane.

As well as a reflective device, an autonomous plane, such as a wall, floor, or ceiling, can be used to renew a space. In Rheinland-Pfalz, Germany, the designers FNP Architekten have remodeled a ruined eighteenth-century pigsty to create a small showroom. The original building had suffered terrible deterioration and was close to collapse. Initially, demolition seemed to be the only option, but due to complex building laws and a very small budget, the retention of the space was made possible. To facilitate this, an independent timber structure was constructed to slip inside the crumbling walls of the shed. The new timber "lining" was assembled off-site, then transported to the site and a crane used to lift it into place. One stipulation was that the new interior could have no contact with the old and that the ruinous quality of the existing was retained, thus giving maximum contrast between the two elements. A new tin roof weatherproofed the structure. The simple quality of the new insertion is reminiscent of traditional vernacular buildings, yet the unpredictable experience of finding a neat timber structure tucked inside an existing ruined, thickly-walled building provides a dramatic statement in the landscape.

In order to attract the attention of a consumer and to stand out from other retail environments, designers will use unorthodox methods to display products and communicate the meaning of a brand. K-Swiss is a sportswear brand that also promotes music events and exhibitions within its retail spaces. 6a architects were commissioned to design a new concept store that displayed their products alongside other significant objects such as books,

Showroom, Rheinland-Pfalz, Germany
Design: FNP Architekten.
The semiruined building is resuscitated through the insertion of a new timber lining.

CDs, and clothing; items that represented
similar brand values. The space also needed
to be able to be transformed quickly from a
working retail space to an open, unbranded
event space. The designers installed a
temporary exhibition system that uses
"found" objects. A library archiving shelving
system is employed, which can be rolled
back and forth on tracks to either open up or
close the space. The five units were reclad
in highly polished perforated steel; this both
reflects the whiteness of the space, while
also affording a degree of transparency. The
units can be transformed within minutes;
they are retracted by sliding along the tracks
and stored in the corner of the room, thus
providing enough space for a performance
or cultural event.

Tactics for autonomous interiors: surface

The surface of an interior is the actual material that covers every object and element. It can confer identity and atmosphere to a space. It is the distillation or the essence of the message that the designer wishes to communicate. Therefore the selection of any number of materials from the millions that are available is an important part of the interior design process.

The tactile qualities of the interior of the oki-ni store in London were undoubtedly important, due to the retailer's unusual method of selling clothes. The store,

designed by 6a architects, is located in the heart of London's tailoring center, Savile Row. It displays clothes as normal stores do and clients can try them on, but once purchased, instead of taking them home, oki-ni mails the clothing directly from their warehouse to the customer. Therefore the impact of the interior of the store was important, and its tactile qualities needed to reflect the qualities and values of the clothing. The interior is realized with a huge, gently sloping Russian oak tray. This is laid diagonally across the floor and rises up the walls to form an overscaled

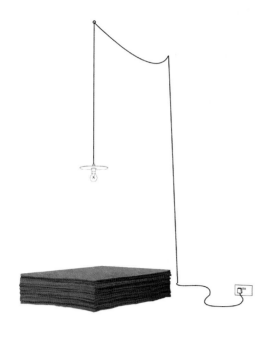

skirting or wainscot. Clothing is then hung from the top of these edges. The tray responds to the vagaries of the existing building by absorbing the irregularities, concealing them on the outside of the straight lines of its walls. The gaps provide spaces for storage and changing rooms. The floor display consists of a series of stacked felt pieces, laid horizontally and stepped to create differing levels of display. Shop assistants can perch on the luxurious felt "benches" and order goods for the customers. The tactile qualities of the interiors combined with the unusual purchasing processes of oki-ni, have created an alternative understanding of the notion of bespoke clothing.

Left: oki-ni store, London, UK
Design: 6A Architects. Clothes and shoes are casually displayed on the freestanding stack of felt panels. Note the items of clothing hanging from the oak upstand that controls and contains the space.

Above: oki-ni store, London, UK
Design: 6A Architects. The simplicity of the interior is illustrated in this concept sketch by the designers.

Right: Kvadrat showroom, Stockholm, Sweden
Design: Bouroullec brothers. The multicolored foam tiles are held together by small interlocking folds.

The Kvadrat showroom in Stockholm, Sweden, was designed by the Bouroullec brothers, who were commissioned to design the interiors using only the company's innovative textile products. In response the Bouroullecs developed a new fabric product: the North Tile. They used this to organize and cover the sensuous interior. The multicolored foam/fabric tile was used in a variety of different ways. It was connected together by a folding system that allowed each tile to be linked through a series of folded "lugs" in order to create larger surfaces or even partitions within the space. This simple method of assembly meant that walls could be easily reconfigured, thus allowing the interior to be changed at a moment's notice. The thickness and quality of the tiles not only

Above: Kvadrat showroom, Stockholm, Sweden
Design: Bouroullec brothers. The stark, industrial showroom space is enlivened by the colorful surfaces.

Below: Kvadrat showroom, Stockholm, Sweden
Design: Bouroullec brothers. With over 100 colors, the tiles can be configured in any pattern or shape.

provided color and warmth to the space, they also delivered good sound absorption qualities and thus a high acoustic rating for inside space. The use of the textiles provided a showroom that projected the company's values and products, while also creating a lively interior that is very much about surface.

Houses need to accommodate their inhabitants in a way that can allow them to work, sleep, and rest. The selection of materials is an important choice for the designer. Next Generation House is a small weekend retreat in the hills of Kumakura, Japan, owned by a timber merchant. The designer, Sou Fujimoto, has created a small wooden pavilion 13 feet by 13 feet (4m by 4m) made from huge blocks of Japanese cedar, stacked and then bolted together for stability. In between the blocks are openings to view out of and also to let light in.

The blocks are stacked in such a way as to allow the owner to sleep, work, cook, and wash within the geometric ordering of the interior. The timber is valued for its stability but also for its surface qualities. In its woodland location, the house is camouflaged by the surrounding trees and hidden by the dense foliage of the hillside.

Above: Kvadrat showroom, Stockholm, Sweden
Design: Bouroullec brothers. The foam and fabric construction of the tiles gives them excellent acoustic properties.

Left: Kvadrat showroom, Stockholm, Sweden
Design: Bouroullec brothers. The vivid foam tiles are a contrast to the industrial nature of the existing building.

Portfolios

Interior design is a vast and wide-ranging subject; many of the different areas are explored in this Portfolios section. The work collected here represents just a small sample of the great diversity and quality of interior design that is currently being built. However, there is one factor that seems to unite the majority of the practices—they cite the existing building as the starting point for their designs, with interiors emerging through the processes of exploration and analysis.

The subject has many different aspects, ranging from projects that are almost architectural—such as the structural remodeling and extension of an existing building exhibited in the work of Pugh + Scarpa—to projects that are on the edge of product design, for example the bespoke furniture created by David Archer Architects.

The practices also range in size. Gensler are a huge firm, employing over 2,000 designers. When commissioned to create a project, they will be responsible for much more than the pure design of the interior space; their work will include the branding of the company, as well as the graphics, advertising, and marketing. Universal Design Studio and Randy Brown Architects are both much smaller practices that retain a real hands-on relationship with the interiors that they create. The designers will be actively involved in the design and the construction of the project, often developing a close relationship with the builder.

The conservation and restoration of an existing structure is an approach that the interior designer is often required to make.

Merkx + Girod have combined the acuity necessary to preserve the quality of the original interior and decoration within a building, with an originality in the interpretation of the character for new use. A sense of history can provide the designer with the motivation for the remodeling of a space; the glamorous, decadent period around the mid-twentieth century has provided the impetus for much of David Collins' work, for example.

The interior can be used for almost every function; indeed there are very few activities that cannot happen indoors. The main categories are covered within this section. The design of retail environments is one of the most prominent areas of interior design, and Lazzarini Pickering Architetti are an experienced design practice in this field. Office interiors also provide a rich source of creative work. Clive Wilkinson Architects epitomize the inventive and resourceful attitude that is often required at the beginning of the twenty-first century as commercial organizations seek to brand themselves through their working environment. The design of the home is often regarded as the domain of the interior designer, the coordination and connection between the disparate parts of the house, combined with the need to specify finishes and furnishing, requires a deep sensitivity and knowledge. Andreé Putman's work for both commercial and domestic spaces exemplifies this approach. Another major aspect of interior design is exhibition design. It is often regarded as a distinct subject in its own right, but a number of design practices create both more traditional interiors and exhibitions. Land Design Studio have developed a strong reputation for the design and development of galleries and exhibitions of distinction and worth.

There are many design approaches that link international practices. Australian firm Multiplicity, situated far from Europe and the USA, approach design in a contextual manner with a great regard for texture and materials and for the character of the existing. This is the same method that British firm Ben Kelly Design takes. Of course, even though the starting point may be similar, the results are radically different.

Interior design is now a widely accepted profession that is appreciated for the beneficial effect it can have on our daily lives. The work of Tarruella & Lopez epitomizes an approach that is both contemporary and timeless. They create spaces that are comfortable and completely appropriate for their use. Casson Mann are a well-respected practice, with a reputation for designing interiors of quality and character. The level of professionalism and creativity that the practice exhibits has done a great deal to create the respectable image that interior design has developed.

All quotations are from conversations between the designers and the authors unless otherwise stated.

Tarruella & Lopez

The practice
Sandra Tarruella and Isabel López met while working for the Spanish architect Pepe Cortés. They had both studied interior design in Barcelona, Spain; Tarruella at the Escuela Diac and López at the Escuala Elisava. They formed Tarruella & Lopez in 1993 and are still based in Barcelona. Most of the firm's projects have been in the traditional areas of interior design such as hotels, retail, residential, and restaurants.

Fundamental concepts
Tarruella & Lopez interiors are characterized by their opulent atmospheres and sumptuous detailing. The duo have worked extensively on retail, hotel, and domestic interiors, but the majority of work they have undertaken is in restaurant design. These spaces require careful organization with a considered selection of atmosphere and surface; the design and placement of the elements and objects required to facilitate this are of utmost importance. They describe their approach as one that does not necessarily follow fashion: "The principle of our work has always been to create timeless spaces, where the luxury is based on comfort, not appearance. This is to create modern spaces based on functional distributions and the choice of materials that are by their very nature and aging with dignity."

When approaching the design for a restaurant, for example, Tarruella & Lopez have four principles by which they design the space, although these could equally apply to all of the social spaces that they design. First and foremost is that the food should be at the center of the design; the

interior must not overshadow the food itself. Secondly the acoustics are as important as the aesthetics. Thirdly context and the local vernacular should be respected. And finally the interior should engage all of the senses. It is this philosophy that is the basis for all of their work.

Key project
Hotel OMM, Barcelona, Spain
Working with the architect Juli Capella, Tarruella & Lopez were commissioned to design the interiors of the Hotel OMM. This chic boutique hotel is situated in Barcelona's Passeig de Gràcia shopping district, near Gaudí's Casa Milà. The exterior of the hotel is striking: the façade is defined by a series of splayed limestone panels that appear to peel away from the main façade. Each panel forms enough space for a small balcony for

the room behind, while at the same time shielding the room from the noise of the traffic and the harshness of any direct sunlight. It also screens the room from the unwanted gaze of the occupants in the buildings opposite.

The public spaces of the interior contrast with the exterior and the suggested discretion of the façade. Upon entrance the reception desk and its back wall are picked out in a bright red, thus making it easily identifiable. The foyer is an open, light-filled space. It is designed around a series of

Below: Hotel OMM, Barcelona, Spain
The generous and sumptuous first floor bar and restaurant are punctuated and ordered by the pyramid-shaped artificial lights.

Right: Hotel OMM, Barcelona, Spain
The carefully placed seating and rugs give the feeling of individual rooms set within the large, open foyer.

direct views through the room that culminate in a small garden, which also acts as the backdrop to the restaurant and bar. The foyer is free-flowing and vibrant, and is populated with a variety of furniture, a mixture of informal and formal, that allows the guests to select a space in response to how they want to interact with each other

and with the room. Rugs are used to delineate each particular cluster or "room" of furniture. Contrast is a very important concept in the space: hard is situated next to soft, large against small, and bright against dark; in one corner, comfortable deep sofas are joined by a single, bright yellow Arne Jacobsen Egg Chair.

Toward the rear of the foyer, and deep into the space, is the Moo restaurant, which is naturally lit by the small courtyard garden onto which it faces. At night, nine pyramid-shaped artificial lights that enigmatically cut through the soffit of the space compensate for the lack of natural light.

Each of the hotel's 91 rooms are individually styled and richly detailed to give a feel of minimalist luxury. On the rooftop, there is a pool and terrace overlooking the city arranged to allow guests to soak up the Mediterranean sun.

Above left: Hotel OMM, Barcelona, Spain
The bathroom is designed as a freestanding element within the hotel room.

Left: Hotel OMM, Barcelona, Spain
The Moo restaurant faces onto a small landscaped courtyard, thus increasing the apparent size of the space and blurring the boundary between inside and outside.

Above left: Viallis Shoes store, Madrid, Spain
The display of shoes is visible from the street. The exhibition stand is placed on an axis with the window.

Above: Viallis Shoes store Madrid, Spain
The freestanding sculptural display object is constructed from rough blocks of wood. This is in stark contrast to the steel panels and the smooth, poured resin floor.

Selected projects
Vialis Shoes store, Madrid, Spain

At just 52½ feet squared (16m), this tiny shoe store required a dramatic installation to make it stand out from the surrounding stores, and to make a statement about its high-quality shoes. The small space is dominated by a freestanding sculptural display stand that is fabricated from huge, sturdy blocks of oak, which are held in a simple steel-frame support. Each block is pivoted from the central support and rotated to form a sinuous wave. This creates the display for the shoes, which appear to be walking across the planks; a simple and effective idea that is unusual and lends movement to an otherwise static object. The rest of the space is finished in a limited, simple palette of mild steel panels and white plastered walls with a white resin floor.

Below: Viallis Shoes store Madrid, Spain
The footwear is displayed in a robust manner .The pivot rotates from the center and allows the shoes to be viewed in a variety of ways.

Cuines Santa-Caterina restaurant, Barcelona, Spain

The Santa-Caterina market has recently been renovated by EMBT (Enric Miralles—Benedetta Tagliabue), making a new dramatic statement with a colored tile roof that folds and wraps over the teeming, bustling market space below. In the corner of the market, Tarruella & Lopez were commissioned to create a restaurant. The proximity of the market influences all aspects of the design. The servery runs from the front to the back of the restaurant and forms the backdrop to the market stalls in the main hall. The other side of the space is dominated by a long timber shelf wall that acts as storage and

Cuines Santa-Caterina restaurant, Barcelona, Spain
The long and open space of the restaurant is framed by the servery on one side, and by the wall of wine and produce on the other.

display for the wine, food, oils, crates of produce, and even cutlery brought from the market. The tables are robust and overscaled, and the experience of eating in Cuines is akin to strolling through the market, while being surrounded by people and fresh produce. The restaurant is a totally appropriate response to the energetic and frenetic surroundings.

Top left: Cuines Santa-Caterina restaurant, Barcelona, Spain
The servery provides the backdrop to the market stalls. The busy and bustling retail space is separated from the restaurant by a thin sheet of glass.

Above and left: Cuines Santa-Caterina restaurant, Barcelona, Spain
The tables are ordered in a linear fashion; the spacing is punctuated with trees. The exposed structure of the roof supports the service elements.

Left and above: Cuines Santa-Caterina restaurant, Barcelona, Spain
The timber shelf wall displays condiments and cutlery. The aesthetic of crates and boxes is borrowed from the adjacent market hall.

Randy Brown Architects

The practice

The practice was formed in Omaha, Nebraska in 1989, and was originally called Randy Brown Interiors. In 1993, the company's name changed to Randy Brown Architects (RBA), and in 1996 the practice created a construction section as an integral part of the business. This allowed RBA to have much greater control over the quality of the built interior. Those working on the actual construction of the design had an intimate knowledge of the project that they were working on, and an affinity with the practice's ethos.

In 1998 Randy Brown founded Workshop, a design/build summer school that aimed to teach students the basic principles of construction. It was designed to encourage students to acquire the sort of knowledge that they would not normally obtain during a formal university education, that is, the experience of actually building something. So the course encouraged the student to spend a very limited time in the studio, and then up to 10 weeks on site, constructing their design.

Fundamental concepts

Randy Brown Architects are a practice with a passion for the intimate manipulation of the technical and detailed elements of a design. They explore the minute and intricate aspects of the materials and fixings and have developed a reputation for the efficient and skilful design of the individual components of an interior. Their approach could be regarded as holistic, in that they consider and control every part of the design. Interior design is, in the opinion of the practice "the design of all things within a space: lighting, HVAC, outlets, doors, stairs, walls, floors, windows, ceilings, furniture, art, plumbing, everything."

RBA begin an interior design project in the same manner as many other practices: they analyze both the site and the client's needs, and then they explore the possibilities and propose alternative designs: "We document everything in a 3D model, we analyze the views, the circulation, where are the doors, etc. Whatever is impacting the space needs to be documented from the beginning. Then the program comes into play—what are the intentions of the client? What does the client want? What is the client about? We research the client or the business and try to amass as much information as possible."

Once the overall strategy has been agreed upon, the practice then begins the in-depth detailed design. Because the designers work so closely with the contractor, there is an exchange of ideas about exactly how the design can be constructed. Long conversations with engineers and other experts ensure that nothing is left unconsidered. Appropriate and innovative choices of materials and their assembly characterize each project. Sustainability and elegant construction methods are of utmost importance and the identity of each project is the result of this care and thought. A major source of RBA's creativity is its understanding of the properties and costs of materials. The practice is skilled at creating unique spaces with limited budgets, such as RBA's own studio, which is also the main residence of Randy Brown.

Randy Brown Architects studio and residence, Omaha, USA

A collection of simple elements creatively used can generate a dynamic interior. A strategically-placed assortment of off-the-peg standard pieces can enliven a bland and uninteresting building. This was the approach taken by the practice for the design of RBA's studio/Randy Brown's home.

In a nondescript 1970s school building in Omaha, Nebraska, RBA has installed an elegant structure to create both a home for Randy Brown and his wife, and an office for four designers. The timber and steel construction was assembled using a selection of readily available materials from the local hardware store. This do-it-yourself aesthetic lends itself to a temporary piece of furniture, a factor that helped Brown to persuade the local council that this structure was furniture rather than a new-build, and hence eased its transition through planning.

The three-dimensional structure acts to split the building both vertically and horizontally; the upper floor contains the private family bedroom and a roof terrace, while the first floor is used for public activities—the studio, meeting room, and the service areas. The stairs, bookcases, the dining/meeting room, and an open sleeping loft are actually situated within the construction. The structure, which incorporated many recycled materials, was built from exposed 2x4 lengths of timber, conduit, plywood sheet, steel, and glass.

As well as wowing prospective clients visiting the studio, the interior was also designed to display the process of its

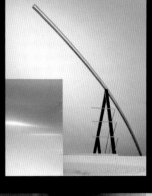

Right: RBA studio and residence, Omaha, USA
The off-the-peg qualities of the installation are contrasted with elegant bespoke details such as the steel balustrade on the upper floor.

Below: RBA studio and residence, Omaha, USA
The new element is designed as though it is a piece of overscaled furniture within the room.

Left: RBA studio and residence, Omaha, USA
The new studio inhabits the double-height space of the school, barely touching the sidewalls of the original building.

Below left: RBA studio and residence, Omaha, USA
The service elements, such as the plumbing pipes, were deliberately left revealed, reinforcing the design aesthetic of exposed details.

Right and below: RBA studio and residence, Omaha, USA
The meeting room is at the heart of the element. The table is supported by a large steel panel that also conceals shelving inside it.

construction, demonstrating what the practice was capable of in a project. The Browns occupied the building during the remodeling, and the design of the container changed as it was being built, as elements were moved around until a satisfactory relationship within the space was reached. The anonymity of the original school building merely provided the shell for the new, dynamic interior.

Selected projects

John Luce Company office, Omaha, USA

RBA created this office for a building and contracting firm who wanted to express their qualities as experts in creative projects. On seeing a shared interest in design and creative construction, the John Luce Company commissioned RBA to create a space that conveyed the energy and excitement of being on site. The brief was for an office interior that appeared as though it was still in the process of construction. The office, which is situated within an anonymous shed-type building, was completed in the familiar RBA language of off-the-peg materials such as precut timber, polycarbonate, ply, glass, and steel; all materials that you might find in a hardware store. The process has been successful; JLC report a greatly increased turnover, some of which is a direct consequence of the dramatic and creative office interior.

Left: John Luce Company office, Omaha, USA
Off-the-peg materials such as ply, steel, acrylic, and air-conditioning ducts are casually juxtaposed with each other to create a dynamic interior.

Top right and above: John Luce Company office, Omaha, USA
The office is organized over two floors with the reception on the first floor and the main office above it. The interior conveys the energy and creativity of the process of construction with the aura of a "work in progress."

120BLOndo office, Omaha, USA

This project is a daring and not uncontroversial version of the standard large steel industrial shed that is so prevalent on the periphery of most cities. Instead of the normal ribbon windows and corrugated walls, the building is dominated by a large sculptural element that rises out from the center of the structure and pushes forward to form an entrance area. The shed is also considerably lower at the rear, as a direct response to the surrounding landscape. The reception is a dramatic, triple-height interior space that was conceived as a series of overlaid panels and materials. RBA have designed a building that stands out from its banal surroundings and makes a creative statement about the intent of the occupiers.

Left: 120BLOndo office, Omaha, USA
At ground level, the reception desk is a much calmer installation. Waiting spaces and circulation routes are clearly apparent.

Above: 120BLOndo office, Omaha, USA
The reception is positioned within a triple-height void. It a riot of surfaces, walls, and venting ducts, all bathed in warm and radiant top light.

Right: 120BLOndo office, Omaha, USA
The dynamic and vibrant interior is visible through the glass and steel entrance box and entices the visitor towar the building.

Poulson Kjeldseth Advertising office, Sioux City, USA

RBA were commissioned to project a new spatial identity for this advertising agency that would promote the company as the most creative among its peers. The robust existing building, a bonded brick warehouse was used as a backdrop to contrast with a series of lightweight installations. The space was organized with a series of static, crisp plasterboard walls, which contrasted with a series of movable fabric panels. This allows the employees the flexibility to create and control their own space. Exposed plumbing pipes, galvanized buckets, air-conditioning ducts, scaffold poles, and steel tread-plate complete this robust and inventive office environment.

Top left: Poulson Kjeldseth office, Sioux City, USA
The monitor in the meeting room is supported by a movable timber and steel arm. This is held in tension by cables that are connected to a galvanized bucket counterweight (out of picture).

Far left: Poulson Kjeldseth office, Sioux City, USA
Exposed pipes and off-the-peg materials such as steel tread plate are used to create an informal, yet serious work environment.

Left: Poulson Kjeldseth office, Sioux City, USA
Crisp white plaster walls contrast with the exposed brick walls of the existing building to create a raw, yet inviting atmosphere.

Above: Poulson Kjeldseth office, Sioux City, USA
Exposed ducts and raw brickwork complete the interior's industrial aesthetic.

Pugh + Scarpa Architects

The practice

Operating in the fields of interior design, architecture, engineering, and planning, Pugh + Scarpa strive to produce work that encompasses aesthetic, environmental, and social concerns. Their work ranges from interior designs, including object design, furniture, and public art, to large-scale educational, civic, and affordable housing buildings and master planning and urban design. Based in Santa Monica, California, the company was founded in 1991 by Gwynne Pugh and Lawrence Scarpa.

Fundamental concepts

Pugh + Scarpa's work is always rooted in its context, both cultural and physical. The practice regards the unique considerations of the original building as highly valuable, something that provides a rich and diverse set of circumstances to draw upon. The analysis of the existing is the study and exploration of the quality and character of the interior, and includes an examination of the form and structure, the history, geography, geology and previous function, all of which can combine to create a rich canvas upon which to create a new layer of design intervention. They have a great reverence for the original building, and strive, if possible, to retain its integrity. They play upon the impact of contrast, of the distinction between old and new, of the disparity that can be created between a worn and weathered shell and the clean and new elements placed within it.

Pugh + Scarpa describe this as a "respect for the structure and bones of our interior spaces, with our built enclosures and shapes lightly touching the original shell, lending the overall experience the sensation of being both in a 'raw' and an 'occupied' space."

They want the original building to be understood, that is, to be obvious, and not to be overwhelmed by the new elements. It is through the analysis of the existing spaces that they feel that they can intervene to create a dialogue between old and new, where both exist in a mutually symbiotic relationship.

The practice strives to create spaces that are calm and encourage the user to become focused and centered upon their task; they "strive to ensure that interior spaces are not oppressive and lacking in daylight." To this end, they often generate long views through the building and beyond its boundary. They also give much consideration to the way that people enter the interiors: "Whenever possible, we design our entry sequences as long processions, so that the visitor may compose himself and enter the office on his own terms. He can take in the architecture and begin to inhabit the space, while collecting his thoughts."

Pugh + Scarpa will typically approach a project by exposing the fundamental character of the original building and then populating the interior with a series of independent structures. "Our efforts tend more toward creating objects within the overall space, placed in such a way that one can still comprehend the overall enclosure— they direct attention to the space as much as to themselves." This creates interiors of exceptional individuality and distinct and specific quality.

Key project

Xap Corporation offices, Culver City, USA

Xap Corporation is an online management resource center for college-bound students. The existing building is a large 22,000 square foot (6,700m) space, situated in the Eric Owen Moss–designed Backslash building. Any new design had to be approved by Moss, and, because Xap were renting the space, any new additions, including mechanical services, could not alter or touch the existing building in any significant way.

Pugh + Scarpa proposed that the new interior should be constructed as a series of freestanding elements that accentuated the qualities of the host building. The digital focus of the client informs the organization of the space. The designers created a 164 feet (50m) long "superhighway" circulation space through the building, from which reception, rooms, offices, and social spaces are all linked. This route invites users to drift right through the space before the need to make contact with workers or other users.

XAP CORPORATION

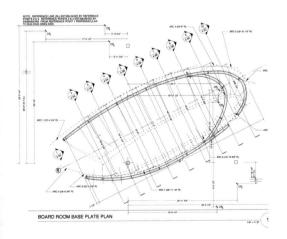

BOARD ROOM BASE PLATE PLAN

Left: XAP office, Culver City, USA
The detailed plan drawing of the meeting room shows the complex process of designing and then fabricating such a sculptural object. Note the sheer number of section lines needed to construct this extremely complex form.

Top and above: XAP office, Culver City, USA
The freestanding meeting rooms are conceived as organic shapes within the orthogonal rigidity of the plan.

...anding objects and elements populate
...erior and allow full visual access to
...ilding's signature clerestory lights in
...of. This allows plenty of natural light
...into the main space. Two sculptural
...elliptical structures dominate the
...one is the boardroom and one a
...ence room. The sculptural rooms are
...l-frame construction, made from
...section steel bar that is left exposed
...outside. In an unusual twist the
...were then rendered smooth with a
...r finish on the inside. Other bespoke
...anding objects, such as a poured
...te reception and contemporary

Above: XAP office, Culver City, USA
The interior of the meeting room is rendered smooth with plaster. The curved walls encourage focus to be placed centrally on the meeting room table.

Top: XAP office, Culver City, USA
The top layer of cladding is removed to reveal the steel frame and insulating material.

Left: XAP office, Culver City, USA
Air movement in such a large interior, which contains so many people and pieces of equipment, is of primary concern. Rather than being concealed, air-conditioning outlets are celebrated as part of the aesthetic.

Above: Jigsaw, Los Angeles, USA
The translucent screen wall of the enigmatic and sculptural main editing suites show whether the rooms are occupied.

Top right: Jigsaw, Los Angeles, USA
The two freestanding editing suites appear to float upon a shallow pool of water within the cavernous shed.

furniture, finish the space. While there is plenty of program crammed into the hall, the feeling is of free space.

Selected projects
Jigsaw Headquarters, Los Angeles, USA

A 5,600 square feet (1,700m) factory space has been transformed to house the headquarters of Jigsaw, a film-editing company based in Los Angeles, California. Usually, editing suites are dark, insular spaces, where natural light and other environmental factors that can be counterproductive for working in are effectively filtered out. However, this can have a detrimental effect for the workers. Pugh + Scarpa have overcome this by treating the two editing rooms as freestanding sculptural objects, positioned in a shallow tray of water, that look like they are leaping from the water. Both are constructed in a similar manner—steel frames clad in lead—but one is finished with ping-pong balls sandwiched between

Above: Jigsaw, Los Angeles, USA
Secondary light filters into one of the boxes via the translucent screen, and into the other through hundreds of ping pong balls.

panes of glass and the other is finished with glass beads. This is an unusual solution, designed to counteract screen glare, and pixellate the view out in the rest of the space. Social spaces are free-flowing areas that invite interaction and relaxation.

Click 3X LA, Santa Monica, USA

Click 3X LA is a digital effects and animation studio situated within an industrial wasteland. The project involved vastly expanding an industrial building formerly used to manufacture residential water heaters. The intense, technologically rich program included Inferno rooms used to create visual effects and computer animation for commercials, TV shows, and large-format movies.

The designers maintained the spatial continuity of the vastness of the space and the industrial character of the building. They then inserted a series of sculptural enclosed rooms to accommodate the needs of the users. These were positioned to create unbroken visual corridors that extended through the entire length of the space. The industrial nature of the original building combined with the expressive nature of the new structures creates a dynamic and dramatic interior.

Top right: Click 3X LA, Santa Monica, USA
Public space between the freestanding elements is expressed with natural light which enters into the building through top lights.

Right: Click 3X LA, Santa Monica, USA
The editing suites and the meeting rooms are playfully shaped in order to animate the interior.

Left: Click 3X LA, Santa Monica, USA
The editing suites are sculptural and dynamic objects in the space.

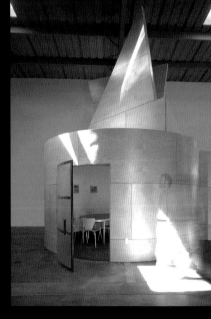

Above: Click 3X LA, Santa Monica, USA
The enigmatic objects are clearly visible through the transparent façade.

Right: Click 3X LA, Santa Monica, USA
The eccentric and dynamic nature of the new elements expresses the practice's ethos.

Multiplicity

The practice

Multiplicity is a practice founded by interior designer Sioux Clark and architect Tim O'Sullivan. The office is based in Brunswick, a suburb of Melbourne, Australia. The company's name was chosen to convey the multitude of professions and disciplines involved in working with the built environment. "Multiplicity" is the result of ideas and hard work from a variety of design professionals in order to realize a successful design project.

Fundamental concepts

The practice's work is characterized by its thoughtful reuse of existing spaces and its careful attention to detail. The designers take on an almost obsessive quality with regards to understanding the buildings they work with. For instance, when working on the Glenlyon church project their obsessions took the form of drawing and surveying the existing building in a massive amount of detail. "It's a form of madness, but our practice spends a great deal of time just

measuring and getting a sense of the space." in-design

Multiplicity's work is essentially domestic in scale. Quite often it involves the reuse of unusual buildings such as warehouses or old churches. These types of buildings often consist of large, open spaces that require careful planning and an attention to detail in order to not obscure the qualities of the host space. Multiplicity also enjoys the "found object" quality of buildings of this type, contrasting elegant new interior design with the original rough and ready surfaces. It is through the careful placement of specific elements and objects that they achieve a balance between old and new, hard and soft, and bright and dull.

Key project
Glenlyon church, Victoria, Australia

A listed building may only be altered in a limited manner. The architect or designer may respond to this challenge by carefully placing new, seemingly ephemeral, elements within the place so that they do not touch or alter the building, but respond to it. This approach was taken by Multiplicity when they converted the Glenlyon church into a family home.

The designers began by making a detailed study of the building; this involved measuring, surveying, and even drawing each individual stone within the building's envelope. Within the capacious hall of the church, Multiplicity installed a large, open architectural structure made from steel, green acrylic, glass, and timber. The vivid construction responds to the shape and rhythm of the existing building in a quite distinct and contrasting language, although the orthogonal nature of the new element is as robust as the original building. The double-height installation contains the bedrooms,

Glenlyon church, Victoria, Australia
The interior of the small church offers a warming presence to the outside wilderness.

bathrooms, and other services in a controlled and ordered manner, thus leaving the more public activities of dining and lounging to the chaos of the old church floor.

The interior is divided by this bright green structure. The smaller area next to the front door is used for relaxing and entertaining guests, while the area on the other side is the dining room and kitchen. The bedrooms, bathrooms, study, storage, and services are gathered together in the complex three-dimensional composition. The study is on the upper level and hangs over the dining and kitchen area, like a modern pulpit.

Left: Glenlyon church, Victoria, Australia
The double-height, freestanding element contains the bedrooms and bathrooms.

Below: Glenlyon church, Victoria, Australia
The space within the living area is carefully controlled in order to create a feeling of intimacy.

The building has not lost its ecclesiastical character: the exterior has a distinctly Gothic Revival style, which has remained unaltered. Indeed, some of the stained glass has been retained. The interior walls have been stripped and painted white to emphasize the exposed roof trusses. The new elements do not touch the old building yet they are derived from the scale and proportions of the host, juxtaposing the new against the old. "We wanted to create texture and relief, something that evokes the past in an abstracted way," explains Sioux Clark.

Below: Glenlyon church, Victoria, Australia
The dining space has a direct connection to the outside through new, fully-glazed doors.

Right: Glenlyon church, Victoria, Australia
The kitchen is situated in the large full-height space beyond the freestanding structure.

Below left: Richmond warehouse, Melbourne, Australia
The intensity of light within the circulation area is moderated by translucent sheets.

Below right: Richmond warehouse, Melbourne, Australia
Direct vertical connections are made through the building with open grid flooring.

Right: Richmond warehouse, Melbourne, Australia
Rectangular grids within the cladding express the orthogonal nature of the building.

Left: Laetitia and Sebastian house, Melbourne, Australia
The rough stone flooring creates an inside–outside ambiguity.

Right and far right: Laetitia and Sebastian house, Melbourne, Australia
The use of yellow mosaic tiling brightens dark and damp areas.

Below and below right: Laetitia and Sebastian house, Melbourne, Australia
The full-height glazed windows allow the living spaces within the house to extend into the garden.

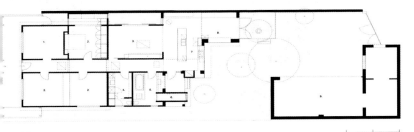

Left and below: Laetitia and Sebastian house, Melbourne, Australia
Note the long corridor that creates a direct link between the front door and the garden.

Laetitia and Sebastian house, Melbourne, Australia

This is another conversion project, but rather than a warehouse, this is an early twentieth-century dairy that has been transformed into a family home. It was originally converted in the 1970s, in a fairly uncompromising and modernist manner. Multiplicity were asked to reconfigure the plan to create spaces that were more functional and comfortable. Due to the limited budget, the project primarily involved dealing with what was there and reworking the existing structure. The designers began by creating a direct relationship between the dining area and the courtyard garden by removing the gable-end wall. This gives an ambiguity to the space—is the courtyard inside or outside of the house? The long bespoke surfaces within the home also contribute to the sense of movement within the space. They seem to slide between one room and the next, which both accentuates the length of the interior and allows the spaces to be used in a flexible manner.

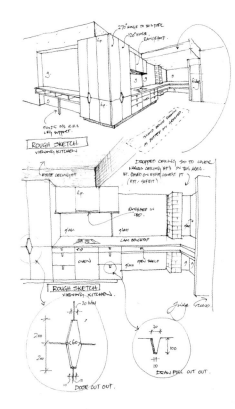

Right: Laetitia and Sebastian house, Melbourne, Australia
The rough sketch has been directly translated into the finished room.

Merkx + Girod

The practice

In 1990, interior architect Evelyne Merkx joined up with architect Patrice Girod and together they worked informally on a series of small-scale and interior projects. Merkx + Girod was formed officially in 1996 with the commission for the ABN-Amro bank headquarters in Amsterdam, the Netherlands. Their work is predominantly interiors or remodeling based, but will draw on the varied expertise in their office, which includes architects, designers, engineers, and draughtsmen. Merkx + Girod employs over 30 staff and is located in central Amsterdam.

Fundamental concepts

Merkx + Girod's work is characterized by bold and striking spatial interventions that are well detailed and appropriately finished. At whatever scale and type of building project they are working on, they always apply a careful and thoughtful sensibility that is appropriate and responsive to the vagaries of the existing building. Their work is filtered through an interior design-led philosophy, meaning that space, light, color, and atmosphere are very important considerations. Their projects show a careful consideration of a suitable identity with which to reflect the occupants of the space. The company has its own materials and models laboratory where research and development into materiality, surface, and the effects of light and material on spaces can be tested. This allows the designers to make some innovative and unusual responses to their projects, allowing time and energy to be spent on the development of new solutions for projects.

Key project
Selexyz Dominicanen bookstore, Maastricht, the Netherlands

Selexyz Dominicanen was created from the merger between three of Maastricht's leading bookstores and is housed in the awe-inspiring setting of a thirteenth-century Dominican church. The building has an interesting history: the Dominicans were driven out by Napoleon in 1794 and, after a brief spell as a parish church, the building had lain dormant for many years, being used as a bike pound until 2007. Its reuse as a bookstore allowed Merkx + Girod to create a space that resonates with many layers of meaning: the rich, semiruinous fabric of the existing building makes an unusual backdrop for the books and a café. The strategy was predicated on the hard mathematics of the project. In order for the store to work, 3,937 square feet (1,200m) of display space had to be found within the church footprint of 2,460 square feet (750m). Originally the clients wanted to drop a new mezzanine floor across the interior of the church in order to increase the floor space. Merkx + Girod resisted this, insisting that the exceptional architecture and height of the space was retained and used to contrast with any new intervention into the space.

Therefore their strategy was to build upward. The solution was a new multilevel black steel walk-in bookcase, situated orthogonally in the main hall of the church. Popular books are placed on the first floor, while academic and esoteric works are kept on the top floors, ensuring a climb for those pursuing elusive or rare books. The journey up through the case allows visitors to move through the stack, a sequence of compression and expansion through the case and out into the open church space. As they climb to the top of the stair they experience the colossal dimensions of the church and are close to the 1619 ceiling paintings by Jan Vessens, depicting saints and sinners from the Bible.

The bookcase is a monumental gesture that matches the grand scale of the church and adds to its dimension, creating views

Top right: Selexyz Dominicanen bookstore, Maastricht, the Netherlands
Low level seating accentuates the ribbed arching within the apse.

Right: Selexyz Dominicanen bookstore, Maastricht, the Netherlands
The top level of the bookshelf provides a marvellous view of the magnificent ceiling.

and vistas across the space. Although huge, the case appears light. Its steel frame construction and black perforated steel cladding counterpoints the mass of the church interior.

The café has been installed in the apse of the church, at the center of which is a large crucifix-shaped table, cheekily reminding the user of the previous function of the church.

Right: Selexyz Dominicanen bookstore, Maastricht, the Netherlands
The huge bookcase element is situated off-center within the nave of the disused church. This creates an open study space in front of it.

Below: Selexyz Dominicanen bookstore, Maastricht, the Netherlands
The rigorous order of the freestanding element reflects the classical language of columns and arches.

Selected projects
Kunsthalcafé, Rotterdam, the Netherlands

On the first floor of the iconic Rem Koolhaas–designed Kunsthal museum in Rotterdam, Merkx + Girod have designed the new Kunsthalcafé. The redesign of the space had to take into account the existing structure and surfaces of the building which are untouchable; this included the light installation on the sloped concrete ceiling by artist Gunther Forg. The strategy for the project was to install a freestanding central bar unit and seating, with reading spaces and tables. The back wall bathroom entrance was also reworked. The series of interior elements are finished in robust materials and placed upon a continuous bright green vinyl floor.

Top left: Kunsthalcafé, Rotterdam, the Netherlands
The new café is situated immediately behind the façade of the building and occupies a strange place beneath the sloping lecture theater.

Top right and bottom left and right: Kunsthalcafé, Rotterdam, the Netherlands
The neon circular lights reflect the organization of the interior.

Concertgebouw, Amsterdam, the Netherlands

The Dutch architect Adolf Leonard Van Gendt designed and built the impressive neoclassical concert hall in 1861. The building is renowned for its excellent acoustics and ornamental design. Merkx + Girod worked on this project for over 10 years, partly restoring the building back to its original splendor and also imposing a

Above: Concertgebouw, Amsterdam, the Netherlands
The concert hall has been restored to its original splendor.

Right: Concertgebouw, Amsterdam, the Netherlands
The decoration of the circulation spaces within the neoclassical building is both sympathetic and appropriate.

new coherent identity on its interior. The central hall had been covered with paint through previous unsympathetic restorations. The designers reworked the hall, picking out details in gold leaf, and using no less than 12 variations on white to give the main hall an understated look. Merkx + Girod also worked on the recital and choir halls and sympathetically upgraded the foyer spaces.

Concertgebouw, Amsterdam, the Netherlands
The decoration is correct and reflects late nineteenth-century neoclassical Flemish interior design.

Universal Design Studio

The practice

Universal Design Studio (UDS) is a practice that works predominantly in the fields of retail and branded environments. UDS is an unusual practice in that its origins lie in the furniture design business of Jay Osgerby and Edward Barber. They found that they naturally became involved with the design of interiors and, from that, with architecture. The practice now employs over 20 architects and interior designers and has offices in London and Melbourne. The company has an extensive list of clients from across the world where they have realized a series of interesting fashion outlets, museums, and workspaces.

Fundamental concepts

UDS's beginnings in furniture and object design have subsequently influenced many of their larger-scale productions. Each project is infused with a subtle yet high regard for the detailing of interiors and the creation of a suitable design language through the selection of furniture and materials. Their initial start within the intense world of furniture design has meant that the practice has retained an interest in the minutiae of detailed design. They are aware of how things are put together and care about the selection of materials and how the junctions are fashioned. Texture and finish are also important, and the practice has developed a reputation for the beautiful quality of the surface finishes within their interiors.

Right and top right:
Stella McCartney store,
New York, USA
The screen, which is
constructed from fine textile
strands, separates the
circulation from the
display areas.

Key project
Stella McCartney store and headquarters, New York, USA

Universal was commissioned to design Stella McCartney's flagship store in the meatpacking district of New York. The converted warehouse was the first store to be opened, setting the house style for a chain of stores across the world. The brief was to design a relaxed environment that provided a respite from the busy city outside. The designers were keen to interpret natural features within the space. For instance, the levels and contours of the floors are continuous and linked to hanging screens that are particularly reminiscent of rushes or grass. The interior is formed as a terrain, for customers to explore.

BarberOsgerby created a glazed tile for the store that incorporates petal motifs with a hexagon, and which builds on the landscape theme of shapes and flowers. The tiles were applied to a long, sinuous entrance wall that wraps around the perimeter of the space.

This pastoral scene contrasts with the interior's sleek, urban furniture and finishes. Exquisite and expensive dresses are displayed in the window on mannequins that are placed on smoked-glass plinths. Reflective chrome sheaths cover existing structural elements. Finely-worked polished steel balustrades guide visitors through the store and help them overcome the change in floor levels. All of these are perched on a white stone floor. The atmosphere is one of rural charm that has been given a sleek, urban update.

Below left: Stella McCartney store, New York, USA
The hexagonal glazed tiles are inspired by the floral motif of the store.

Below: Stella McCartney store, New York, USA
The mannequins appear to float above a watery glazed strip that separates the store interior from the outside.

Selected projects
Canteen, London, UK

The design for the Canteen restaurant was based on the optimism of mid-twentieth-century design and the classlessness of public buildings, such as schools, libraries, and town halls. UDS have embraced this vision with a collection of beautifully-crafted pieces of timber furniture. The organization of the space is very simple—the dining furniture is arranged in rows, with the kitchens and bar secreted behind a wall. A floor to ceiling glass wall that runs the whole length of the restaurant ensures that the space is naturally lit and thus imbues the interior with an open and honest quality. The painstakingly manufactured furniture informs the character of the interior. The emphasis is on simple, honest materials (oak, marble, linoleum, cork, tweed) that ensure design longevity and reflect the quality of the food on offer.

Below: Canteen restaurant, London, UK
The view from outside is evocative of an Edward Hopper painting.

Above: Canteen restaurant, London, UK
Corner booth. The materials are deliberately understated.

CANTEEN

Eliden, Lotte Department Store, Seoul, Korea

On the fifth floor of Seoul's Lotte Department Store, UDS have created a concession for the women's fashion retailer, Eliden. The space is organized using a series of open screens made from etched glass. The design of the screens is influenced by traditional Korean textile, and gives the impression of loosely woven bamboo canes. When these are lit from above and below they provide a shimmering backdrop to the products on display. The rear wall of the unit is constructed from white textured panels. These have an abstracted flower motif on them, which, when viewed through the translucent screens, gives the impression of continuous movement.

**Left: Eliden, Lotte
Department Store,
Seoul, Korea**
The etched glass screen
blurs the view through
the interior.

**Below left: Eliden, Lotte
Department Store,
Seoul, Korea**
The floor finish acts to control
the position of the display
elements within the store.

**Right: Eliden, Lotte
Department Store,
Seoul, Korea**
The white textured panels on
the rear wall of the space
echo the nature of the
products on sale.

**Below right: Eliden, Lotte
Department Store,
Seoul, Korea**
Although appearing chaotic,
the store interior is organized
in a systematic and ordered
manner.

...ndrée Putman's life is intimately entwined with her work; to know one is to also understand the other. She is a self-taught designer, and brings to her work a mixture of influences ranging from contemporary music and dance to art, architecture, and literature. Born in France in 1925 into a wealthy family, Putman originally studied music and was awarded the highest prize at the Paris Conservatoire's Prix d' Harmonie. Realizing that she would not make a virtuoso, she moved on from the Conservatoire to become a writer and an artists' agent, writing about the bohemian Paris scene of the 1960s and buying and selling prints by painters she admired. She formed the style consultancy Mafia and then, in 1979, founded Écart, a studio that initially reworked found objects from the flea markets of Paris but which later went on to reissue classic pieces of furniture by such designers as Robert Mallet-Stevens and Eileen Gray. It was then a logical step for Putman to design her own interiors, which led to commissions for retail spaces, hotels, and other interior designs across the world. Today Putman is still designing and creating bespoke, elegant interiors.

Putman's work is characterized by its classic and refined qualities. The transient and temporal nature of most interiors work is overlooked and instead projects are built to last. Each project is viewed as an enigmatic statement that will endow each space with a unique identity. Putman's training in music and her experiences as a journalist, design consultant, and stylist have informed her knowledge of harmony, balance, and the combination of objects and elements in space. Each of her projects could be viewed as an essay in opulence and in the use of exquisite materials. The work is timeless: "My interiors are simple, but not impersonal, serene but not cold, tempting but not opulent, charming but not nostalgic, they are refined but not restrictive. Basically, I always try to reconcile poor and rich materials. It is an antighetto and nonconformist idea about the arrangement of space, the light, and the elegance of details. Some people calculate and constantly search for the latest trends, but that's not my objective. I use my feelings and my mind to access a bazaar of different styles and concepts."

Left: Morgans Hotel, New York, USA
The walls, ceiling, and floor of the lobby transform the checkerboard motif into a series of geometric patterns. The monochromatic interior is enlivened by the colorful and atmospheric lighting.

Top right and right: Morgans Hotel, New York, USA
The checkerboard monochromatic tiles used in the hotel bathrooms are also translated to become the pattern for the blankets on the beds.

Key project

Morgans Hotel, New York, USA

In 1984 Putman designed the original
Morgans Hotel in New York, one of the first
"boutique" hotels. Putman reinterpreted the
hotel in 2008, updating its classic, timeless
qualities. The monochromatic interior of the
hotel is a translation of the iconic bathroom
of the original. The most striking of the hotel
spaces is the lobby: the black-and-white
optical effect of the checkered sandstone
floor—which was inspired directly from the
original bathrooms—dominates the main
aesthetic of the space. This pattern is used
throughout the hotel, from the signage to
the blankets on the beds.

The new project also includes an interactive art installation commissioned by Andrée Putman by French art group, Trafik. It is loosely based on the work of the artist M.C. Escher, who created optical illusions of fabulously unreal landscapes. This piece is constructed from LED displays, which were placed on the ceiling in the lobby, and the light filtered through a sheet of white Barisol, which is a flexible plastic. The installation projects a range of images and patterns that the hotel guests can select and then record the ones that they like the best.

Left and below, left and right: Morgans Hotel, New York, USA
The interior design of the hotel rooms is an essay in opulence and sumptuousness.

Above: Morgans Hotel, New York, USA
The lighting in the lobby is designed to respond to the moods and requirements of the hotel guests.

handelier that hangs vertically through the space, linking the three levels of the building. is constructed from a metal mesh, and is

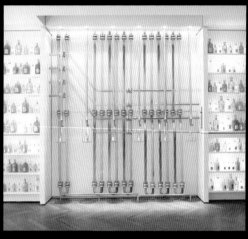

Below, left and right:
Le Spa Guerlain,
Paris, France
Many innovative methods of display are used in the interior. The main space is dominated by a huge chandelier constructed from metal mesh and lit in a way that transforms the humble material into a sensuous and exotic surface.

Top: Le Spa Guerlain,
Paris, France
The treatment areas are dominated by a circular motif, which is used in the design and arrangement of the furniture and the large mirrors.

Anne Fontaine boutique and spa, Paris, France

Fashion designer Anne Fontaine is renowned for her crisp, white women's shirts; every season she produces hundreds of this classic fashion staple. She is also the owner of over 70 stores worldwide, and in 2007 commissioned Andrée Putman to work with her on her new flagship store in Paris' fashionable rue St Honoré. The new store would include her trademark shirts but also branch out into beauty treatments and a spa. The space is organized over three floors, and Putman and Fontaine decided that water would be used as a unifying feature. A wall clad with Hainaut bluestone forms the backdrop for a waterfall that spills between the store and the spa. Retail is on the first and second floors and the spa is in the basement. On the first floor the famous shirts that made Fontaine's name are displayed in an elegant set of glass display cases. A staircase, which is also lined with the bluestone, takes the client to the spa. Here clients can spread out on sumptuous beds or bathe in the deep graystone Jacuzzi pool. The resultant spaces are controlled and elegant, something that Putman always strives for in her work: "I try to remind myself how much a peaceful place can ensure mental comfort. The visual context enables [people] to obtain the feeling of wellbeing. We often forget the immense peace that emerges from an unloaded room, soft and human, where the concern for calmness is the most important thing. What I find stimulating is making a place where one can calm down and feel good without being anesthetized by an overbearing cosiness."

Blue Spa, Hotel Bayerischer Hof Spa, Munich, Germany

Putman's design for this hotel spa complex was made with her trademark attention to materials and details. The space exhibits a quiet dignity combined with ergonomic consistency. The aesthetic is almost nautical: water of course dominates the design, but the interior language could have been taken from an ocean liner—thin sections of birch wood are connected to simple tubular steel frames, while uncomplicated wooden loungers and minimal detailing provide the spa with an open and airy feel. The building is topped by a swimming pool that is under a retractable glass roof that can be closed in seconds. The space is a haven for relaxation and pampering.

and the Delano Hotel in Miami. In 2008 the practice was awarded the Interior Architect of the Year award by the UK-based *Building Design* magazine.

Fundamental concepts

Interior design for leisure and retail environments can often be considered a shallow area of the discipline, motivated only by considerations of surface and look, and stimulated by financial gain. David Archer's work offers an alternative to this in that each interior is carefully thought out and has a consistent, substantial concept underpinning its execution. Central to all of the work is a commitment to refined craftsmanship and a rigorous approach to detailing. Typical to all of the projects is the application of highly refined interior elements that imbue the space with an atmosphere of luxury.

Working on the refurbishment of period and heritage properties, the practice has developed an expertise in designing powerful contemporary interiors, which harmonize with their historic settings. Bespoke lighting and furniture are designed to create atmospheres unique to the setting and

This 150-cover restaurant is situated on Brewer Street in central London. The interior was designed to contrast with the bustling streetscape outside by providing a calm and cool environment in which to dine upon the high-quality Japanese food. The interior of the restaurant is designed to elevate and enhance both the presentation and consumption of Japanese food, in particular, sushi. The Japanese narrative is highly developed. It begins with the initial concept with inspiration drawn from traditional temple design and modern neon and glass Tokyo street imagery. These themes are combined and reworked to create different dining "zones," each being influenced in different ways by the spaces, patterns, and materials of contemporary and traditional Japan.

The restaurant is situated on the first and basement floors of the existing building. The first floor space consists of a centrally ordered dining area surrounded by a bar that runs the full length of the space. The back of the bar is a timber wall that is detailed to give an illusion of water when light falls upon it. The ceilings are clad with tatami mats, arranged within the grid of beams. The depth of each beam is elaborated upon with translucent glass panels, a contemporary interpretation of traditional Japanese sliding doors. The lower-level dining space is dominated by a 33 foot (10m) long sushi bar. The fish is displayed under glass, as though each piece is an elegant piece of jewelry. The counter is sunken so that diners seated before it can observe the sushi-making process that unfolds in front of them.

Aaya Restaurant, London, UK
Natural light is filtered into the interior through translucent glass that provides a cool and calm environment.

The detailing of the restaurant is elegant and thoughtful. Bespoke furniture has been designed by Edward Barber and Jay Osgerby exclusively for Aaya. It consists of a series of pieces that are carefully scaled and respond to the space and to each dining event. On the first floor, seating is either individual at the tables or as "banquettes." These are made from oak with pink lacquer rails and anthracite leather upholstery. The tables are solid oak with white glass tops. The basement seating is also in oak but finished in white leather, while the sushi bar stools are completed with black leather. A floral motif abstracted from a traditional kimono print is used as a decorative element throughout the scheme. It has been redrawn and embroidered in silk to provide lampshades, and has been routed out of dark oak to add decoration to the wall panels. Lighting is also carefully used with warm light refracting through panels of ribbed bronze glass, evoking the nighttime streetscape of downtown Tokyo.

Right: Aaya Restaurant, London, UK
The vertical circulation is wrapped with translucent glass. Flashes of colored lighting are filtered through this screen and evoke the busy streetscape of Tokyo.

Below: Aaya Restaurant, London, UK
Elegant, bespoke stools line the long bar, reinforcing its linear qualities. The length of the room is punctuated by large, overscaled lampshades.

Below left: Aaya Restaurant, London, UK
The floral motif of a kimono has been etched into the timber door of the service spaces.

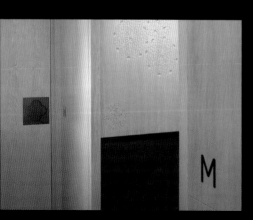

Right: Ink Bar, Bournemouth, UK
Lighting is carefully considered in the hall. A series of pendant lights hang from the ceiling illuminates each table, reinforcing the volume of the grand space.

Below: Ink Bar, Bournemouth, UK
The main dining hall is organized with a series of centrally placed orthogonal booths. This arrangement is reinforced by the long, linear bar and row of chandeliers.

Selected projects
Ink Bar, Bournemouth, UK

The inspiration for the style and the name of the Ink Bar comes from the building that it occupies: the Grade II listed Seal and Hardy Building in Bournemouth, UK, former home of the Bournemouth Echo newspaper. The bar itself occupies the newspaper's former reception area, hence the name, while this beautiful art deco building provided the stylistic influence for the design of the new interior. The streamlined and angular qualities of the retained exterior were transported into the interior. The Ink Bar is not only a venue in its own right, but also provides a point of arrival for diners at The Print Room brasserie.

The space is organized in a regular orthogonal manner with the stained timber bar counter at one end, leaving the main space for high bench tables. These are dark, but the undersides are painted buttercup yellow to accentuate the height and relieve the potential heaviness of so much dark wood. The walls are painted white with dark wainscoting, which could be slightly oppressive, but art deco style mirrors and other ornaments relieve the weight. The exits and other opening are painted the same yellow as the undersides of the table, adding a quirky sense of the ridiculous to the interior.

Below: Ink Bar, Bournemouth, UK
The intimacy of the smaller dining room is shattered by the full-length wall of mirrors that endlessly reflect the room.

Below right: Ink Bar, Bournemouth, UK
Neon within the window reveals. Color is used just once in the space, which creates an intense and dramatic statement.

Below far right: Ink Bar, Bournemouth, UK
The retention of original features such as the art deco clock reinforces connections between the new interior and the original building.

Above: Ink Bar, Bournemouth, UK
The diagram shows the orderly and efficient placement of the various activities within the interior.

Above: Isarn restaurant, London, UK
Although the interior is a long, thin room, each place setting is made intimate through lighting and materiality.

Above right: Isarn restaurant, London, UK
The linearity of the room is punctuated by large, overscaled light shades and hanging pendant lights. Note the sailcloth blinds in the roof of the conservatory.

Above, far right: Isarn restaurant, London, UK
The bar reinforces the length of the thin room. It is placed at the most narrow point within the space.

Below: Isarn restaurant, London, UK
The long, narrow space is well organized around the central spine of circulation.

Isarn restaurant, London, UK

This restaurant occupies an extraordinary site that is just 13 feet (4m) wide, but 82 feet (25m) long, culminating in a small exterior courtyard. David Archer Architects accentuated the linear qualities of the site by offering long perspective views all the way through the space. To achieve this, facilitating elements, such as the bar counter, the servery plus all the tables and chairs, were distributed at the edges, thus leaving the central spine of the space free for circulation and visual connection.

The indoor and outdoor dining areas are linked by a conservatory hung with a natural sail cloth in a tent-like ceiling. This effectively allows the space to continue undisturbed from inside to outside, thus once again exaggerating the tremendous length of the restaurant. This is a daring strategy—it could possibly be intimidating for the customer to have to walk through the length of the space—but it is actually an intimate and cheerful experience.

David Collins Studio

The practice

David Collins Studio has evolved over 20 years from a small interior design practice specializing in private residential projects into a studio of over 50 people, with offices in London, New York, and Buenos Aires. The practice is the company behind some of the world's top interior architecture and multidisciplinary design projects including leading international retail, bars, restaurants, hotels, yachts, and spas. They take a comprehensive approach to design, where interior architecture, furniture, lighting, and graphics coexist and interact, seamlessly producing a strong comprehensive vision for each individual project.

Fundamental concepts

David Collins Studio are unashamed modernists who exhibit an obsession with the control of every detail of the design. They are keen followers of the clean and minimal expression exhibited by Ludwig Mies van der Rohe, Eileen Gray, and of course, Le Corbusier. They strive to create interiors that are absolutely unique to each particular client, and it is this understanding of the needs of those who will be using the interior that forms the starting point of every project, as David Collins explains: "I know it's a bit of a cliché that interior designers say that they start at the 'bones' of the project, but I also tend to start at the personality of a project, or the building, or the location—and it is all of these that combine to give you direction on how to achieve something special."

Once the studio has established the direction that the project will take, then the earnest design and control of the details begins. David Collins himself has often quoted Mies van der Rohe's maxim "God is in the Details," and so the practice explores the technology of the intimate detailing of the materials and junctions. The resultant interiors are highly sophisticated places that are rich yet minimal with opulent materials but without overt decoration.

The designers find inspiration in historic architectural styles, not as things to be copied, but as something that they will explore and use to stimulate the design of an interior. David Collins explains: "Sometimes a Romanesque or baroque interior, even a Gothic interior, can inspire me to something that ends up being quite contemporary."

Right: Bob Bob Ricard restaurant, London, UK
The highly decorated, compartmentalized interior is reminiscent of an American diner. The sumptuously upholstered booths are ordered by numbers, which are inlaid into the flooring.

Top right: Bob Bob Ricard restaurant, London, UK
The monogram of the bar is made from brass and set into the terrazzo flooring.

Key project

Bob Bob Ricard restaurant, London, UK

This restaurant is an eccentric kind of Parisian brasserie-cum-New York diner in central London. The design is a contemporary interpretation of an art deco interior. The materials are rich and opulent, with the use of gilt and mirrors exaggerating the sense of sumptuousness. David Collins Studio have employed their usual obsession with control over every design detail, even to the extent of specifying the waiters' uniforms.

The dining space is divided in an ordered and regular manner to create booths.

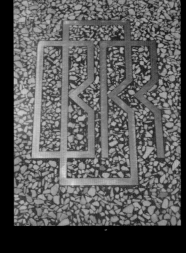

Bob Bob Ricard restaurant, London, UK
Interior atmosphere is created through the extensive use of rich and opulent materials. More intimate dining spaces are secreted behind velvet curtains. The main dining room is rigorously organized into a series of orthogonal booths. Dining here is a theatrical experience.

The banquet seating in the more open, day-lit area is covered with bright blue leather with brass edge detailing. This creates a bright and cheerful atmosphere of busy formality—guests are encouraged to interact with each other and enjoy the bustling character of the room. The red dining room is also organized with booth seating, yet it is much more intimate and suitable for the more relaxed nature of the long evening dinner. The space is artificially lit and the red leather banquettes are sumptuous and luxurious. The walls are covered with a red patterned silk finish and the ceiling is low, thus reinforcing the intimate atmosphere of the interior.

Bob Bob Ricard is the sort of place in which it would not be surprising if a 1950s movie star was to stroll in, sit down, and order breakfast.

Callas Café and Restaurant, Budapest, Hungary

The Callas Café and Restaurant is named for opera diva Maria Callas, and appropriately so, since it sits on Andrassy Boulevard in Budapest opposite the opulent nineteenth-century State Opera House. The café's interior design is obviously influenced by late nineteenth-century decadence combined with David Collins Studio's interest in all things art deco.

   The main open dining space is treated in a very simple manner: the bar is at one end with the dining booths and loose seating occupying the rest of the space. The walls and floors are treated in a straightforward way: the walls are white with dark wainscoting and the floor is made from white and brown stone. It is the attention to the junctions and details that provide the interior with an aura of luxurious decadence; the ceiling vaults are gilt-edged, the chandeliers are made from ornately detailed brass, and the seats are covered in embossed leather. This results in a space that is both contemporary and yet appears to have existed for over a century; it feels as though it has a history, as though it is an experienced occupant of this florid city.

Callas Café and Restaurant, Budapest, Hungary
The cavernous grand hall has been designed to evoke the past as much as the present. Its elegance provides the perfect backdrop to eating and drinking.

The London NYC, New York, USA

Texture is an important element in all the work of the David Collins Studio, and this project shows them manipulating it at their best. The hotel is predominantly pale brown and cream in color; individual spaces and rooms have been defined using different materials and finishes. For example, within the dining room, beige marble is placed next to cream leather, which is situated within an off-white room lined with pale gold walls. The tablecloths are just white, the crockery is coffee-colored, and the carpet is fawn with buff streaks. All of this could combine to become insipid and bland, yet the texture of each material is strong and individual and therefore the room becomes a wonderfully welcoming collection of warm finishes and surfaces.

Top: The London NYC, New York, USA
The grid of the ceiling is reflected in the layout of the tables to provide an ordered and efficient space.

Above: The London NYC, New York, USA
The geometry of the floor and ceiling surfaces in the lobby creates a unified and distinct interior space. Note the dominance, and thus importance, of the long reception desk.

Left: The London NYC, New York, USA
The atmosphere of the dining room is softened by the use of texture combined with pale materials.

Left: The London NYC, New York, USA
The far end of the lobby is dominated by an overscaled hearth. While it is not functioning or used to heat the room, its dominance offer a focal point to the space.

Below: The London NYC, New York, USA
The long and glamorous bar is illuminated by a large lighting sculpture. Many different textures and materials are combined to create a bar of opulence and distinction.

Ben Kelly Design

The practice

Ben Kelly formed Ben Kelly Design (BKD) in London in the mid-1970s. One of the company's earliest projects was the commission from Malcolm McLaren and Vivienne Westwood to design the infamous Seditionaries boutique in London. Described as "a Clockwork Orange Betting Shop," the store was also a rehearsal space for the Sex Pistols. During the 1980s and 1990s, BKD completed three interior projects in Manchester, UK, that are now seen as iconic designs: The Haçienda nightclub (1982), the Dry 201 bar (1989), and the Factory Records headquarters (1990).

Fundamental concepts

Although the practice was influential during the time of punk, the work of BKD really epitomizes the postindustrial generation who, having survived the bleakness and deindustrialization of the 1970s, embraced the concept of warehouse living and partying. The Manchester projects represent the types of interiors that were vanishing from society at that time. Big, open warehouse spaces were no longer used for industry but for raves and nightclubs, and the Haçienda was probably the most famous of them all. The stripped-out factory aesthetic proved to be highly influential and for a while became much copied.

BKD always claims that the original building is the generator of the interior, that their work is merely an interpretation of what is already there, and to a certain extent that is true. Many of the BKD interiors still contain the remnants of the building's previous occupation, indeed these relics or residues of earlier use are often used for decoration or ornament. However, it is the masterful understanding and elucidation combined with the careful placement of new elements that makes the work of BKD so successful. Kelly describes his work as something that has integrity far beyond just surface consideration, he regards it as something that is "very close to architecture but it's not architecture," that actually has little to do with surface treatment, but has its basis in the manipulation and control of space.

Each BKD project is characterized by a number of particular qualities. Inventive and unusual responses to an existing building are combined with sensitive and innovative planning and the use of exceptionally hardwearing materials. The practice is known for the use of a myriad of materials and finishes. They will experiment with different versions of the same design proposal, trying it out with one material after another. They will also evaluate and test the worth of familiar products in unfamiliar positions, for example, in BKD's own studio bright orange plastic buckets are used as lamp shades. This approach makes BKD an antidote to the chain-store aesthetic of "one size fits all."

Key project

The Haçienda, Manchester, UK

The Haçienda nightclub was completed in 1982 and was BKD's largest project at the time. It was without precedent, and has subsequently achieved iconic status as one of the greatest cultural and hedonistic spaces of the late twentieth century. Recommended to the owners of Factory Communications by their Art Director, Peter Saville, Ben Kelly was

**Left: The Haçienda,
Manchester, UK**
Architectural promenade. The
visitor would pass through a
series of different spaces
before arriving at the heart of
the nightclub. The tread-plate-
lined foyer was the first part
of the sequence. Note the
Factory Records serial
number carved into the door.

**Below: The Haçienda,
Manchester, UK**
Industrial motifs inform the
decoration within the interior.
The screens were used for
the projection of movies.

**The Haçienda,
Manchester, UK**
The distinctive interior was
defined through its bold use
of color and materials.

Traditional materials such as
timber were placed directly
against unusual elements
such as traffic posts and
hazard strips.

given free reign to rework the ex-yachting
showroom in central Manchester to create
a bespoke nightclub and music venue.

The club's presence on the street was
almost nonexistent; the clubber would pass
through a small, dark door into a tight lobby,
and from there into a slightly larger area,
described by BKD as "a massive cathedral-
like space which is heightening and
magnifying this experience, which you
become overwhelmed in once you're in
there, it takes you over." This is typical of
BKD's work, where the movement is linear
and is very much about the circulation of
people through the interior. Spaces are
designed in series, as a progression of
scenes for the user to inhabit, each
connected to the last through the themed
use of materials, textures, and colors, but
with a distinct and identifiable atmosphere.

The interior was left very much in its found
condition, even to the extent of retaining the
massive roof light—an element that is not
really much use in a nightclub where any
daylight is usually carefully excluded. Just
about everything was painted pigeon blue and
the identity of the interior was completed by
the use of found objects such as traffic
bollards and cat's-eyes. The exposed
steelwork received a layer of brightly-colored
hazard stripes in yellow, red, and black. An
industrial interior for the postindustrial society!

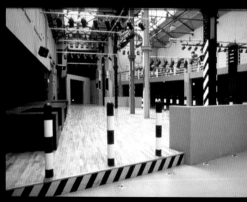

**The Haçienda,
Manchester, UK**
The nightclub was a
hardwearing and industrial
space. The cavernous space
was once a showroom for
boats. The large hall was left
intact and the bar, dance
floor, stage, and DJ box were
organized within it.

Selected projects
Bar Ten, Glasgow, UK

Located down a narrow, dark alleyway and discreetly hidden away from the busy shoppers on Princess Street (Glasgow's main retail artery), Bar Ten is known only to the select few who can find this unusual and intimate space. The bar occupies the first floor of a tall, turn-of-the-century industrial building. BKD opened up the front of the bar to the narrow alley by inserting full-height windows, allowing the limited amount of natural light to filter into the interior of the space. The interior, which is wider at the front than the back, is dominated by three cast-iron columns that run off-centre, front-to-rear through the bar. This created two distinct areas; the counter was placed in the smaller part and the seating area in the larger. The bar counter was formed from a solid block of terrazzo that curves up from the floor and reinforces the integral robust quality of the space. The exposed air-conditioning ducts that hang to the ceiling and run through the space tie the whole interior together. Bar Ten is a vigorous and forceful response to a strong and uncompromising situation.

Top right: Bar Ten, Glasgow, UK
The structure of the existing building dominates the first floor. Found materials are juxtaposed against new interventions to create a distinctive and characterful interior.

Middle right: Bar Ten, Glasgow, UK
The L-shaped space is split into two distinct areas: the bar area and the main seating space. The long air-conditioning duct links the front and back of the space.

Bottom right: Bar Ten, Glasgow, UK
Glazed bricks, bold colors, and exposed steel beams complete the uncompromising industrial aesthetic of the interior.

Gymbox Covent Garden, London, UK

BKD broke the mold of traditional, sterile white and clinical gym environments by creating a new vibrant space to work out in. This gym is housed in a former movie theater, and the original structure was used as a backdrop for a series of colorful installations. Taking center stage is a full-size boxing ring, providing an arena for fitness through fighting. Again BKD have used a strong palette of materials to complement the raw character of the existing environment. Brightly-colored vinyl finishes contrast with the untreated concrete walls of the original buidling. BKD also experimented with the use of colored light, as particular areas are highlighted through the use of neon and the entrance is a glowing white-and-yellow box. The designers have embraced the concept that boxing is no longer a sport for a few passionate individuals and created an inviting, vibrant atmosphere for all.

Top and above: Gymbox Covent Garden, London, UK
A very simple and direct font used on all the signage signals the appropriate spaces to the visitor.

Left: Gymbox Covent Garden, London, UK
The boxing ring dominates the center of the space and provides the focus for the interior.

Top left: Gymbox Covent Garden, London, UK
The glass-fronted dance studio hangs in the center of the space. The highly-engineered character of the interior is reinforced through the exposed ducts and pink-edged steel frame.

Left: Gymbox Covent Garden, London, UK
The shiny and polished surfaces of the changing rooms reflect the clientele's narcissistic preoccupations.

Top right: Gymbox Covent Garden, London, UK
Lighting animates the circulation around the subterranean space, highlighting the textured qualities of the found surfaces.

Above right: Gymbox Covent Garden, London, UK
Terraces of equipment line the room, focusing attention on the boxing ring.

moving to the USA to work for Gehry. His move into interior architecture and design was not planned: "My involvement in interior architecture was accidental. I was working on large building structures for Gehry, and had a side job designing the interiors for Chiat\Day advertising. When I started my firm, they were the first people to give me work." Interior Architecture Now

CWA has completed interiors for many well-known brands and worked for clients from a variety of business sectors, including advertising agencies, banks, broadcast and media companies, and arts organizations. The practice is also not afraid to work on projects in the more "traditional" interior design areas of retail and restaurant design.

Fundamental concepts

Much of CWA's work has been in the field of office design, including new workspaces for Pallotta TeamWorks (2002), Google (2005), TBWA\Chiat\Day (1998), and Mother (2004). Each of these projects involved the creation of innovative and appropriate spaces for the workers, but also effectively communicated each client's ethos. CWA use witty ideas to create these spaces. Off-the-peg objects such as shipping containers are stacked on top of one another to create office space in an industrial shed in the Pallotta TeamWorks

design ideas were allowed full reign within the old brick structure of the historic Royal Laundry Building. The large interior is broken down into separate work and meeting spaces through the use of modular, brick-like elements. Foam-block walls are used to create one conference room, while a second is formed by a modular, honeycomb-shaped structure. These elements allow for flexible use of the space and also make an apt allusion to children's building blocks. Visitors to the office walk through a topiary gate in the shape of the iconic Mickey Mouse ears. Such playfulness is characteristic of CWA's work and, along with their appropriate use of materials, allows them to communicate their clients' ideas.

Pallotta TeamWorks, Los Angeles, USA
Private and individual rooms are created in the cavernous space by the use of colorful cargo crates.

Key project
Pallotta TeamWorks headquarters,
Los Angeles, USA

Based in a large, anonymous warehouse, this building interior was designed to house the headquarters of Pallotta TeamWorks, a charity-events organizer. After an initial cost analysis, it became apparent that the client's budget would not even stretch to adequately air-condition the building. Therefore the whole of the building had to be designed and built on a shoestring budget. To save money, an off-the-peg set of solutions was devised. Major structural alterations to the existing building were avoided to save both building time and expense. The main work areas were created using ready-made objects. Tents were erected to optimize environmental performance. These created smaller enclosed spaces that were individually conditioned, thus reducing the need to environmentally control the whole building. Their corners were pinned back and secured by shipping containers that also housed private office spaces. Other huge crates were painted bright orange and stacked on top of one another; some were also glazed

at the short-end to allow light and air into the offices. Blue shipping containers were placed on the first floor in order to demarcate the edges of the workspaces, and social spaces such as the café were contained in these crates.

As well as cutting costs, this lo-tech approach to the project communicated the client's philosophy with regards to promoting sustainable living and intelligent reuse of the world's existing resources. CWA's thoughtful and appropriate solutions won them many awards including the USA national AIA Award in 2004.

Below: Pallotta TeamWorks, Los Angeles, USA
Ready-made objects provide a dynamic and creative atmosphere.

Above and right: Pallotta TeamWorks, Los Angeles, USA
The reception desk is an opened map of the world to reflect the global aspirations of the company.

Selected projects
TBWA\Chiat\Day headquarters, Los Angeles, USA

This huge warehouse building, which was redesigned as an office space for advertising agency TBWA\Chiat\Day, was one of CWA's earliest projects. The interior is entered via a series of large bridges that were designed to remove the visitor from everyday life and make them feel like they were entering another world. The office was one of the first to blur the boundary between work and lifestyle. The interior consists of a series of "events" based around a main "street." There is a basketball court, a central park, billboards, and "neighborhoods" of workspaces. The bland exterior of the warehouse hides an animated, interior "cityscape" workspace.

Above: TBWA\Chiat\Day, Los Angeles, USA
The interior is expressed as a vivid street scene.

Below: TBWA\Chiat\Day, Los Angeles, USA
Movement and circulation animate the static interior spaces.

Paperfish, Los Angeles, USA

WA proposed a total design concept for this elegant seafood restaurant. The company designed the interior right the way down to the staff uniforms and the glassware, and even suggested Paperfish as the restaurant's name. The interior was conceived as a series of pure white curves and waveforms, evoking the sinuous shapes of fish and water. These appear to randomly float through the space, but they actually control and organize the internal arrangement, forming the walls and holding the lights and air-conditioning. This purity is complemented by the bright red and orange soft furnishings, which are vivid within the cleanness of the interior.

Left: Paperfish restaurant, Los Angeles, USA
The sinuous waves of the soffit evoke the feeling of water and movement.

Top right: Paperfish restaurant, Los Angeles, USA
The upholstered red wall dominates the far space of the restaurant.

Right: Paperfish restaurant, Los Angeles, USA
The continuous counter surface of the bar unites all of the disparate areas of the restaurant.

Casson Mann

The practice

Casson Mann are a highly influential practice who have been at the forefront of interior design for the last quarter of a century. They have a reputation for creating interiors of taste, quality, and sophistication. Their work is understated and modest, while still being utterly contemporary. They create distinct interiors that combine thoughtful ideas with cutting-edge technology. Casson Mann was founded in 1984 in London and is the partnership of Dinah Casson and Roger Mann. Casson Mann specializes in museum and exhibition design, however, the practice is also involved in other interior work, such as offices and domestic spaces.

Fundamental concepts

Casson Mann regard the interior as a narrative, that is, a space that is occupied, experienced in time, and viewed while in motion, rather than as a static and single focused situation. They strive to create environments that possess identity, that express feeling, and that reflect the intent and aspirations of those occupying them. Exhibition and installation design is by its very nature ephemeral; the changing nature of spaces and exhibits combined with the expectations of the visitors often leads to the design of interiors that must capture the imagination and attention of the viewer.

The practice argue that "…interior design at its best is the creation of an environment, or series of environments, that reflect, express, identify, and make real feelings that are often intangible. It is powerful: it can change mood, temperature, emotion—and behavior. It can be liquid and responsive, or solid and commanding."

Casson Mann approach each project in the same manner: by thoroughly investigating

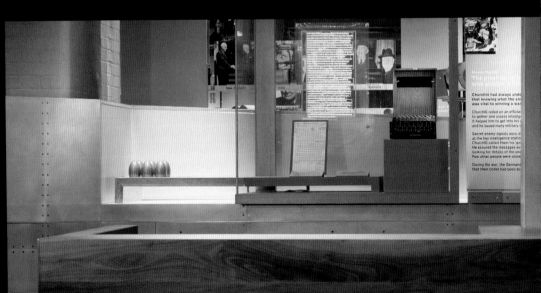

the site, the brief, and the needs and expectations of the users. They regard this analysis as "… a process of examination, deconstruction, lateral thought, reconstruction, critical review, further deconstruction, reconstruction, and so on". This leads the practice to create interiors that are distinct, individual, and, most of all, appropriate.

Key project
Churchill Museum,
Cabinet War Rooms, London, UK
Casson Mann were commissioned to design an exhibition that would represent the whole of Sir Winston Churchill's life, including his political career and personal life, his successes and failures, and, of course, his finest hour as British Prime Minister during WWII. The exhibition is housed, most suitably, in an underground room, the site of the government's wartime

bunker. The museum is connected to the Cabinet War Rooms, which are arranged in a strict and linear manner. The designers decided to contrast these rigid spaces with a looser, less prescribed arrangement for the Churchill Museum.

The subterranean space is dominated by a series of steel columns that are, of course, unmovable. Within this space, the exhibition of the life of Churchill was loosely divided into five sections, with each chapter depicted on a raised plinth that was woven diagonally through the space. Some plinths evade the columns while others simply absorb them and thus appear more rooted

Left: Churchill Museum, London, UK
A sense of history. The exposed rivets and other joints provide the interior with a period feel.

Right: Churchill Museum, London, UK
The robust exhibition display reinforces the bunker-like quality of the space.

in the space. The plinths, which are color coded and lit in different ways, communicate the mass of information attached to each era of Churchill's life.

At the center of the space, and forming the backbone of the exhibition, is the Lifeline, a 49 foot (15m) long interactive table. This contains the Churchill Papers, which were bought for the nation in 1995 and contain an estimated one million documents—from his childhood letters to his speeches and final writings. The table brings this archive to life by allowing visitors to access information directly while also acting as a counterpoint to the looser, more intuitive exhibits that are spread around the space. The table provides a digital experience of an analog age, allowing visitors to access Churchill's diary and open folders of news and events by touching the interactive surface of the table. Thirteen networked computers portray thousands of pages of information, documents, animations, and images.

Left: Churchill Museum, London, UK
The Lifeline is expressed as a strategic diagram.

Right: Churchill Museum, London, UK
Surface pattern is juxtaposed with plain screens of text.

Selected projects
Stanislavski Museolobby, Moscow, Russia

The Museolobby is a unique lobby space dedicated to the memory of Konstantin Stanislavski, the creator of the Method Acting system. It is also the entrance area to the new offices for property developer Horus Capital, which were also designed by Casson Mann. This unusual space combines the reception to the offices and a media center with information on Stanislavski. The space is clean and stark, everything is apparent and expressed with clarity and passion, just as Stanislavski would wish. The space is double-height; the missing floor plate is visible behind translucent screens. The steel columns are large and almost comical, they are so obviously structural. The reception desk is a reflective box with an ornate table printed onto it, symbolizing the nature of its task. The interior is an appropriate response to the nature and function of both the user and the man that it is dedicated to.

Stanislavski Museolobby, Moscow, Russia
The entrance space is shared between the Stanislavski museum and the offices. It has to appear to be both professional and creative.

Camouflage exhibition,
Imperial War Museum, London, UK

Inside the cavernous hall of the Imperial War Museum, Casson Mann designed a temporary exhibition to communicate the connections between the worlds of art and the military in the development of camouflage. The exhibition considered the importance of camouflage to the military and also showed how camouflage has had a direct influence on art and fashion. The exhibition is designed around the basic concept that camouflage is about disguise. The designers devised the exhibition as an abstracted landscape that was folded and cut its way through the walls of the existing space. Ironically this created a landscape of display spaces that allowed the normally hidden to be viewed, for connections to be made that were not normally available, and for the whole space to be connected in a radically different manner. The disparate collection of objects, from models of ships using "dazzle" camouflage inspired by the cubists to one-off fashion pieces, were then placed amid the landscape of plinths and display cases.

Great Expectations,
Grand Central Station, New York, USA

Exhibition design allows the designer to be expressive and mischievous; the limited time span of the interior can stimulate excessive playfulness and risk taking. Great Expectations was an installation with the aim of promoting the best of Britain's products and services. Its location was New York's Grand Central Station, a place which people generally just hurry through. Casson Mann created a startling statement that was designed to stop people in their tracks. The installation took the form of a 164 foot (50m) long table, which was situated within one of the station's busy lobby areas. Upon this enormous horizontal plane was a banquet of products and artifacts, which were lit from below. Chairs were loosely arranged around the table to suggest a meal and to entice interaction with the busy passersby.

Horus Capital office, Moscow, Russia

The designers have again used a creative approach to the design of property developer Horus Capital's Moscow offices. The brief was to create a new open-plan working culture for the company. The idea of transparency was taken very literally by the designers—they placed the management in cellular glass offices, which are situated at the center of the office floor.

The interior is organized by a long timber runway, which reaches from the chairman's office to the boardroom, where it actually becomes the conference table. Elements and objects are attached to it on its journey through the interior. In addition, this long timber plane creates a direct connection between this level and the floor below, which holds the Museolobby, a project also designed by Casson Mann (see page 227). The office's reception area has an interactive reception desk, which reacts and changes with the approach of visitors.

Top left: Horus Capital office, Moscow, Russia
Printed glass provides privacy for the internal meeting room.

Bottom left: Horus Capital office, Moscow, Russia
Circulation spaces are enigmatically lit to evoke the feel of moonlight.

Top right: Horus Capital office, Moscow, Russia
The rhythm of the windows provides the impetus for the organization of the workspace.

Bottom right: Horus Capital office, Moscow, Russia
The existing space was sufficiently large enough to contain a two-story insertion.

The practice

Lazzarini Pickering Architetti were established in 1982, in Rome, Italy, and have developed an international reputation for continuously innovative design. Their work is highly original and conceptual, and encompasses many areas of interior design, retail and restaurant design, interior architecture, and pure architecture. Like many interior design practices, the studio is multidisciplinary and overlaps with many other design disciplines such as product and graphic design. The practice is headed by Italian designer Claudio Lazzarini, and Carl Pickering who is originally from Sydney, Australia.

Fundamental concepts

Lazzarini Pickering Architetti made the deliberate decision to base their practice in Rome, away from the Milan-centric hothouse of Italian design; this allows them to maintain a contemplative and reflective distance from that stressful world. It also allows them to focus on context and environment without having to be overly concerned with fashion or current trends. Contextualism, which is at the heart of Lazzarini Pickering's work, is an approach that is increasingly being taken by contemporary design practices. It is the examination of the site and the surrounding area, and then allowing the analysis of the situation to influence the design of the new interior. Lazzarini Pickering Architetti describe their approach thus: "We believe our projects must be influenced by the 'genius loci' or 'spirit of place' of the different cities and regions where we build, by the architectural and decorative traditions of that place. This does not mean slavishly copying but the reinterpretation of this in a contemporary way for the third millennium."

Although context is very important to the practice, Lazzarini Pickering's work is firmly rooted in the modernist tradition of rigorous, well organized, functional spaces. Their work takes these principles and combines them with thoughtful and elegant elements such as furniture, materials, and light, to create pure and rational spaces with a human scale and an intimate atmosphere. Their work ranges from traditional interior projects such as residential and retail designs, through to more unusual assignments, such as the interiors for luxury yachts. Each project is characterized by a considerate design and the appropriate use of furniture, light, and materials.

Key project

Fendi showroom, Paris, France

Lazzarini Pickering were commissioned to design the concept and the space for upmarket brand Fendi, a chic retailer of clothes, shoes, and bags. They designed a basic pattern of ideas for the brand that could then be rolled out in stores across the world and adapted to the particularities of different sites. The designers devised a series of pieces of furniture, each with a particular geometry, but which are differentiated by the use of materials: dark wood, wax-finished iron, prism mirrors, and glass tops. This furniture was designed in response to the philosophy and brand logo of the company (a pair of interlocking F's); these pieces would personify the brand and act as a suitable backdrop for the merchandise. As the designers explain,

"The idea was not to fill the spaces with sales furniture as in most boutiques, but to create an abacus of architecturally-scaled structures that could also be used for display; a panel, shelving, and table system. Each boutique was a unique configuration of these elements that depended on the specific character of the site."

**Fendi showroom,
Paris, France**
The stainless steel box structures not only provide places for display but also encourage the visitor into the dark recess at the rear of the store.

The space for the Paris showroom is on three floors of a tall, turn-of-the-century building. Like many retail spaces positioned on streets that charge high rents, the showroom occupies only some of each floor plate, sharing space with other stores and exclusive apartments. Fendi occupies half the first floor, while the other half is used for another store and to provide access to the upper floor apartments. In response to this, the designers opened up a central void through the space and connected up the different levels by linking each floor with a stair. The stair folds and winds through the void, also acting as a platform for viewing through the space. The void and the stair are then populated by a series of display elements—the geometric furniture designed to represent the brand. The open-sided boxes radiate out from the void and stair space and inhabit the rest of the shop, uniting the different areas of the space while barely touching the walls of the building. Mirrors are deployed to exaggerate the length of the space and to accentuate the appearance of sliding planes and boxes displaying Fendi's trademark bags. The clothes, bags, and shoes are then displayed on the furniture, either being folded across the boxes or placed inside.

The façade of the building, in particular the windows, are lined with display cases

Top left: Fendi showroom, Paris, France
Linear elements encourage movement within the store.

Bottom left: Fendi showroom, Paris, France
Vertical circulation occurs at the moment of intersection.

so that the interior is disguised from the outside. The new stairs and display elements are treated as an autonomous element within the space. By disguising the form and structure of the host, and by placing new elements within the space, the designers revel in the autonomous qualities of their existence yet they become site-specific as they respond to the vagaries of the existing building.

Above: Fendi showroom, Paris, France
Gaps and fissures between the display elements provide long views through the volumes of the space.

Left: Fendi showroom, Paris, France
The store has a sense of continual movement.

Selected projects
Villa, Positano, Italy

Lazzarini Pickering refer to each project as "site-specific portraits of clients." This is true of the reworking of an eighteenth-century villa set in the fantastic landscape of the Amalfi Coast in Italy. The interior of the space has been opened up to provide a series of comfortable spaces for relaxing and dining. The integrity of the original villa has been retained through the preservation of key architectural details, such as columns and arches, but spatially the building is now much more modern. Many walls have been removed, thus also removing the idea of individual rooms. And so Lazzarini Pickering Architetti has created a free-flowing, multilevelled series of spaces. These are tied together with a floating plane, which slides through the building, and acts variously as a table, a lighting platform, a floor finish, and wall decoration. The old and the new exist together in this sophisticated interior.

Opposite: Villa, Positano, Italy
Surface decoration accentuates the space's three-dimensional qualities.

Above and below, left and right: Villa, Positano, Italy
A richly decorated multifunctional linear element links the living space with the dining room.

GAS Eatery and Supplies, Melbourne, Australia

The clients' names—Giuseppe, Arnaldo, and Son—have been used to supply the new name for Melbourne-based restaurant GAS. Lazzarini Pickering combined elements of the traditional Italian trattoria with a rational, modern aesthetic. The designers, in an amusing postmodern statement about the function of the interior, have hung a huge image of an Italian Renaissance building behind the modern glass façade of the building. The interior is completely different, and as such slightly unexpected: it is long, thin, dark, and populated with fairly aggressive pieces of fixed furniture. The space is black and subdivided loosely into circulation and dining "rooms." This allows for a series of static spaces in which to eat, and then separate busy circulation spaces. In stark contrast to the blackness of the interior, each of the individual dining spaces is elaborately decorated with Sicilian tiles. Different tiles are used to differentiate the different spaces. This creates an extraordinary and quite spectacular interior.

Left: GAS, Melbourne, Australia
Visitors travel through a patterned tunnel.

Opposite: GAS, Melbourne, Australia
Richly-decorated tiles identify the distinct areas within the restaurant.

Left: GAS, Melbourne, Australia
The printed glass façade is the calm foil to the sumptuous interior.

Above: GAS, Melbourne, Australia
The reflective quality of the façade provides a great contrast with the opulent interior.

Gensler

The practice

Interior design is a discipline that can be practiced by large, multidisciplinary organizations, companies that offer complete bespoke packages of services including architecture, urban planning, consultancy, and project management. Although it had its beginnings in the USA, Gensler now has offices across the world, employing over 2,000 professional designers. Their work incorporates all scales of creativity, from the design of a wine bottle label to the planning of a new urban district. Art Gensler founded the company in 1965. Although he trained as an architect, he is widely credited with elevating the practice of interior design to professional standing. He is a Fellow of the American Institute of Architects and of the International Interior Design Association, and a professional member of the Royal Institute of British Architects.

Fundamental concepts

While it is difficult to characterize a particular aesthetic or distinct design language in the work of a practice that is so global and diverse, each project that Gensler undertakes reflects a commitment to the requirements and culture of the client and to sustainability. Gensler have in the region of 2,000 clients, ranging from large and small companies, to profit and nonprofit organizations.

LSE, London, UK
The sculpture within the atrium links the separate floors of the Exchange. The interior has a high-quality, professional character.

Key project

London Stock Exchange, London, UK

The existing 1960s Broad Street location for the London Stock Exchange was too small, overly compartmentalized, and fostered an inhibited working style that was restricting the business of the Exchange. The relocation to new offices in Paternoster Square allowed Gensler to reshape how the 300-year-old Exchange functioned and how its staff operated.

Gensler redesigned the interior of the Eric Parry–designed building to create a more open and flexible workspace, one which can reflect and react more quickly to changes in the global financial markets. Based around the building's existing atrium, Gensler organized the interior around a series of "hubs" or places of contact for the workers and their clients. The main reception was configured to provide glimpses of the live broadcasting studios, allowing visitors to experience this important aspect of the Exchange's delivery of real-time market intelligence to the local and international financial community. Conceived as the public face of the Exchange, the Media Centre includes modern multimedia facilities, radio booths, and four broadcasting studios used for daily transmissions by the ABC, BBC, CNBC, CNN, and Sky News networks.

Many of the center's facilities are also available for hire all year round, including a business center, a 120-seater auditorium, two presentation suites, and two syndicate rooms equipped with state-of-the-art technology. The actual working spaces were designed to foster knowledge sharing, with over 320 people working together on the third floor alone. To further increase interaction, the center of the typical workplace area was transformed in an elliptical area called The Hub, which provides a variety of spaces for informal meetings. All meeting rooms at the Exchange share the same high-quality design vocabulary and

LSE, London, UK
Semiprivate, breakout spaces punctuate the intensity of the interior.

attention to detail and are grouped in distinctive areas: The Avenue (five presentation suites), The Forum (two presentation suites as part of the Media Centre), The Recess (two rooms providing support for prepresentations and conferences), and The Base (a business center created for support functions to the presentation suites). Staff and clients also benefit from a contemporary dining area, named The Foundation.

The new workspace is designed to be a transparent, open, and an enhanced environment that allows its workforce to work in a modern way. In the eight-story atrium, The Source, a kinetic sculpture by the collaborative artists Greyworld, consists of 729 suspended blue spheres that independently move up and down, reflecting the dynamics of the market.

Top right: LSE, London, UK
Full-height glass windows provide a view into the media room.

Middle right: LSE, London, UK
Movement is accentuated by the curved walls of the meeting rooms.

Bottom right: LSE, London, UK
Informal meeting areas are scattered throughout the office.

Selected projects
Burberry headquarters, London, UK

Burberry's new headquarters in London brings together 850 staff under the same roof. The building is organized around an atrium that links all seven floors of office space. The first floor opens on to the street and is framed by tall glass windows etched with the latest Burberry advertising campaign. The reception is backed by a large screen that shows the latest catwalk shows.

Inside each office space, Gensler have structured the interior to allow for flexible working. Long, clean workbenches allow for hot desking, and rows of computer stations complement the modern and

Top: Burberry headquarters, London, UK
The uncompromising quality of the new elements contrast strongly with the textured character of the original building.

Left: Burberry headquarters, London, UK
Breakout balconies suspended over the atrium provide informal places to sit.

Above: Burberry headquarters, London, UK
The reception area has a formal, professional quality.

functional work space. The identity of the interior is derived from Burberry's iconic trench coat, with natural colors used for the floors and walls. On the top floor, the creative director's office is flanked by both the design studios and the cutting tables. This is where new ideas are tested and developed. The creative director's office overlooks the River Thames and has two balconies which can only be used once clearance has been gained from the ominous yet striking MI5 headquarters across the river. The openness of the interior and the connections between spaces allow staff to communicate freely and connect throughout the building, a situation which Gensler advocated by incorporating state-of-the-art video conferencing systems and telecommunications networks, allowing for regular company addresses by the CEO.

Hakuhodo Head Office, Tokyo, Japan

Hakuhodo is the second-largest ad agency in Japan, and it asked Gensler to develop an image that was creative yet corporate, dynamic and reliable, cool, and also frenetic. Gensler's approach was to create a dramatic public area at the center of the office. This contains the main reception floor, the executive floor, the cafe, the library, and a university. This was based on the central uniting concept of "Ugoku, Deau, Tsukuru" or "Move, Meet, Make."

All these new areas are cool and calm, and are united by the strong visual sense of space. The furniture is deliberately low, thus allowing the visitor to look beyond the foreground, across the busyness of the office and into the spaces beyond. Here the designers have then intentionally placed carefully designed elements and objects for the eye to focus on—these may be the reception, an advertising display, or sometimes even a view out of the building. The low furniture is an eclectic mix of colors and shapes, which imbue these spaces with a casual, almost informal, atmosphere.

Burberry headquarters, London, UK
The rigorously orthogonol showroom provides an uncompromising environment in which to display Burberry's chic products.

Edelman office, London, UK

Gensler were commissioned to create the working environment for the London office of Edelman, one of the world's largest PR firms. The solution had to encompass a number of different attitudes and identities. Edelman company needed to communicate an approach that was both professional and creative, trustworthy and slightly off-the-wall, that showed that they were able to think in a dynamic manner, but still be in complete control.

The method that Gensler took to the project was to create a highly flexible environment, one which could rapidly change to reflect the changes in the business needs. From the reception area with the concierge, the gallery, bistro bar, meeting area, and library to the open work areas, very little in the interior is permanent, nearly everything is movable. The furniture and fittings are all bright and contemporary, very high quality and extremely durable. Thus reorganization is an easy process of just moving the furniture around. The 25,000-square-foot (7,620m) office provides a dynamic and engaging work environment.

Above: Edelman office, London, UK
The colorful screens create a joyous and happy atmosphere in the office.

Left: Edelman office, London, UK
The artificial light, which is filtered through the chandeliers, provides a focus to the meeting tables.

Land Design Studio

The practice

Based in London, Land Design Studio was formed in 1992 by Peter Higgins. Their work is predominantly concerned with the design of exhibitions and interiors that represent their clients' requirements through the use of sophisticated communication technologies combined with pragmatic design solutions. Peter Higgins is the Professor of Experiential and Narrative Design at the highly prestigious Central Saint Martins College of Art and Design, London.

Fundamental concepts

Wit, humor, and an engaging playfulness characterize many of Land's projects. The interpretation of source material for exhibitions and design work is always conducted in a rigorous and rational manner. The overlapping of other disciplines, such as graphics and communication media, is always present in their work. Each project also shows a fascination with new technology and the willingness to communicate ideas and messages. Narrative and movement is always a fundamental part of any project, and is sometimes the actual starting point of the design process. "We have found at the early stages that our fundamental objective is to extend and articulate the primary information contained within the client content brief that has been prepared by varied representatives such as curators, researchers, interpretation departments, educationalists, and even brand managers. The initial conceptual design response provides preliminary proposals for the narrative sequence, communication and media protocols, operational and functional planning, and even issues that impact on the funding business and marketing strategies."

Land Design Studio have established strong collaborative partnerships with people from associated disciplines, including researchers, writers, time-based and new media developers, graphic designers, artists, business planners, DDA consultants, and a new wave of sound and lighting designers, all of whom are commissioned to provide appropriate creative and technical support. This allows the practice to build a specific and talented team for each project, one which is absolutely suited to solving the design problem, rather than just using whoever was least busy in the office.

Land Design Studio work at the cutting edge of design innovation and invention; they have a reputation for reliability and originality, which is at the core of their design approach.

Key project
The British Music Experience,
The O2 arena, London, UK

Land Design Studio were one of the first
collaborators to be appointed to work on
this museum project, therefore their
involvement was much greater than is
normal with this type of work—they were
key instigators in the formation of the
project. They were involved with the content
development team, all of whom were
formidable music experts drawn from the
industry and music journalism.

The site was irregular and difficult, so the
first design decision was to create a clean

**The British Music
Experience, London, UK**
The exhibiton design contains
a number of different ideas
for ways of communicating
popular music.

central circular space with perimeter pods. Each pod represented a defined period of musical history and had an entirely different graphic treatment; this helped to provide a changing ambience in support of the distinctive music. The use of digital interactivity was extensive; installations allow the visitor to investigate the very geography of the music, interrogate aspects of music transmission, and play back through object collections. There is even

an interactive exhibition to teach willing participants how to dance.

The designers explain that: "Our starting point to create the organizing principle was predicated on the concept that the diverse range of visitor expectation should be reflected in a very free-flow mechanism with extensive layers of information. We want to encourage self-discovery rather than lay out a prescriptive didactic journey."

Top left: The British Music Experience, London, UK
All visitors are provided with headphones that allow them to experience an individual journey through the complexity of the museum.

Above and right: The British Music Experience, London, UK
The visitors can participate in the exhibition through the use of interactive display elements.

Left: The British Music Experience, London, UK
The exhibition is a series of tableaux that communicate the different eras of popular music.

Selected projects

The Golden Age of Couture:
Paris and London 1947–1957,
V&A Museum, London, UK

The launch of Christian Dior's New Look clothing range in 1947 marked the beginning of a momentous decade in fashion history, one that Dior himself called the "golden age." For this exhibition, which drew most of its objects from the Victoria & Albert Museum's own collection, Land's "design scenography" presented one of the most glamorous decades in fashion history.

Starting with the impact of Dior's New Look, Land designed an exhibition that explored the manufacturing process in a filmic streetscape of glass display cases. These were placed in front of a changing panorama of a city scene. "It was as if the famous ateliers had been deconstructed and distributed to create an urban setting with a transforming projected backdrop cyclorama," explain the designers.

The penultimate gallery featured a large show case installation with a soundtrack by Mantovani that provided the grand setting for 35 ballgowns including those worn by the Queen, Margot Fonteyn and Audrey Hepburn. This very static display was enlivened by a huge slow-motion abstract video projection that was shot inside the ballroom of Osterley House.

The exhibition was designed as a narrative that explored haute couture from its earliest days to the late 1950s, when the leading couture houses had become global brands.

Top: The Golden Age of Couture, V&A Museum, London, UK
A period atmosphere was created within the gallery to complement the era of the clothes.

Far left and left: The Golden Age of Couture, V&A Museum, London, UK
The Mantovani soundtrack complemented the display of ballgowns. The fashion timeline was displayed in a clear and concise manner.

Playzone, Millennium Dome, London, UK
The Playzone was one of 14 zones within the Millennium Dome, the controversial project that was built in London to celebrate the advent of the year 2000. The content within the Dome was divided into themed areas: Who We Are, What We Do, and Where We Live. A selection of well-regarded architects and designers were commissioned to design each section and Land Design Studio were approached to create the The Playzone. It was situated in the What We Do section, alongside Work, Rest, Talk, Money, Journey, and Learning. The objective was to develop an interactive experience that would engage and entertain a broad-based audience.

It was expected that up to 30,000 visitors per day would visit the pavilion, so it needed to be able to process large amounts of people in a meaningful and enjoyable manner and leave them with a lasting and positive impression. Land Design Studio created a freestanding pavilion that the visitors could walk through. Circulation,

or physical movement, was at the heart of the experience; everything had to be appreciated while moving through the pavilion. The entrance ramped up, so that the visitor could get an overview of the complete installation, and they were then led through a series of projected installations to an area of interactive digital mechanisms. The process was deliberately difficult to engage with—the visitor was expected to have to make an effort and not simply to wander around in an unfocused manner. "As with all of our work the planning exercise is fundamental in responding to people movement, dwell time, and sequence, and as an observation we have discovered unlike the golden rule of interior design that often we do not create spaces for relaxation and hedonistic comfort."

Playzone, Millennium Dome, London, UK
The interactive display cases have a playful and exuberant quality.

Bibliography

Books

Adaptations: New Uses for Old Buildings. **Philippe Robert. Princeton Architectural Press, 1991.**
This book presents a series of well-written case studies using unusual and rare examples of the reuse of existing buildings from across the world.

Architectural Voices: Listening to Old Buildings. **David Littlefield and Saskia Lewis. John Wiley & Sons, 2007.**
A poetic study of how historical traces can influence the manner in which a building is converted.

Architecture in Existing Fabric: Planning, Design and Building. **Johannes Cramer and Stefan Breitling. Birkhäuser, 2007.**
An ambitious study of the process of altering existing buildings.

Architecture Reborn: Converting Old Buildings for New Uses. **Kenneth Powell. Rizzoli, 1999.**
Organized along the various functions of interior design, the book shows a series of case studies of the reuse of existing buildings.

Basics Interior Architecture: Drawing Out the Interior. **Ro Spankie. AVA Publishing, 2009.**
A series of illustrated case studies examining the various methods of representing interior space.

Basics Interior Architecture: Form and Structure; Basics Interior Architecture: Context and Environment; Basics Interior Architecture: Elements and Objects. **Graeme Brooker and Sally Stone. AVA Publishing 2007, 2008, 2009.**
These three books form part of a five-part series examining the processes of interior architecture and design.

Building in Existing Fabric: Refurbishment, Extensions, New Design. **Christian Schittich (Ed). Birkhäuser, 2003.**
A series of case studies that illustrate different approaches to remodeling.

Carlo Scarpa: The Complete Works. **Francesco Dal Co, Giuseppe Mazzariol, and Carlo Scarpa. Electa, 1984.**
The complete works of the great Italian designer, known for his sensitive and careful reuse of existing buildings.

The Condition of Postmodernity: An Enquiry into the Origins of Cultural Change. **David Harvey. Blackwell, 1990.**
A very readable, thorough treatise on the development of the condition of postmodernity and how it affected not just the world in general, but also design and architecture.

The Decoration of Houses. **Edith Wharton and Ogden Codman, Jr. B.T. Batsford, 1898.**
Probably the first book to address the design of the interior as an intellectual and separate subject.

Drawing for Interior Design. **Drew Plunkett. Laurence King, 2009.**
A useful and practical resource for students covering all aspects of drawing interior spaces.

Flesh: Architectural Probes. **Elizabeth Diller and Ricardo Scofidio. Princeton Architectural Press, 1994.**
The work of the New York-based designers and architects is used to illustrate the preoccupations and issues of contemporary design.

Foundations of Interior Design. **Susan J. Slotkis. Laurence King, 2006.**
A wide-ranging look at all aspects of interior design from writing contracts through to case studies of projects.

A History of Interior Design. **John Pile. Laurence King, 2000.**
Charts the various ideas and forms in design history.

An Illustrated History of Interior Decoration: From Pompeii to Art Nouveau. **Mario Praz. Thames & Hudson, 1982.**
A very thorough journey through the history of the subject. The brilliant introduction took 18 years to write, so was not included in the first edition of 1964.

In Detail–Interior Spaces: Space, Light, Materials. **Christian Schittich (Ed). Birkhäuser, 2002.**
A comprehensive series of contemporary case studies well analyzed and drawn.

Inside Architecture. **Vittorio Gregotti. The MIT Press, 1996.**
A concise, insightful examination of the role of modernism in the late twentieth century.

Interior Architecture. **John Kurtich and Garret Eakin. Van Nostrand Reinhold Company, 1993.**
The seminal overview of the ideas and developments in the design of contemporary and historical interior space.

Interior Architecture Now. **Jennifer Hudson. Laurence King, 2007.**
A useful and colorful selection of numerous interior designers from across the world.

Interior Design of the 20th Century. **Anne Massey. Thames & Hudson, 1990.**
Still the best and most relevant outline of the recent history and profession of interior design.

The Interior Dimension: A Theoretical Approach to Enclosed Space. **Joy Monice Malnar and Frank Vodvarka. John Wiley and Sons, 1992.**
An exhaustive exploration of the theoretical approach to the design of interior space.

Intimus: Interior Design Theory Reader. **Mark Taylor and Julieanna Preston. John Wiley & Sons, 2006.**
A scholarly and academic collection of excerpts from seminal works on interior theory.

Modern Architecture since 1900. **William J. R. Curtis. Phaidon, 1982.**
A well-written and comprehensive overview of the main architectural movements of the twentieth century.

On Altering Architecture. **Fred Scott. Routledge, 2008.**
A series of great essays that discuss the reworking of the existing. Subjects range from interior design through to architecture and painting.

Privacy and Publicity: Modern Architecture as Mass Media. **Beatriz Colomina. MIT Press, 1996.**
The representation of space, especially through photography, has always been an interesting subject. The author explores the works of Le Corbusier and Adolf Loos through their attitudes and responses to the representation of their work.

Raumplan Versus Plan Libre: Adolf Loos and Le Corbusier. **Max Risselada (Ed). 010 Uitgeverij, 1991.**
A catalog from an exhibition, this book examines the two differing space-planning strategies of Le Corbusier and Adolf Loos.

Re-Architecture. Old Buildings/New Uses. **Sherban Catacuzino. Thames & Hudson, 1989.**
An examination of the reuse of existing buildings using case studies from across the world.

Rereadings: Interior Architecture and the Principles of Remodelling Existing Buildings. **Graeme Brooker and Sally Stone. RIBA Enterprises, 2004.**
An exploration and analysis of the process of reworking existing buildings and a theoretical discussion about the nature of the interior, using case studies from across the world.

Sub-Urbanism and the Art of Memory. **Sebastien Marot. Architectural Association Publications, 2003.**
An exploration of the contextual approach that the designer can take.

Thinking Inside the Box: A Reader in Interior Design for the 21st Century. **Interiors Forum Scotland. Middlesex University Press, 2007.**
A collection of essays and works from academics across the world on the latest ideas and issues in interior architecture and design.

Translations from Drawings to Building and Other Essays. **Robin Evans. AA Publications, 1992.**
Historian Robin Evans' writings covered a wide range of concerns about design such as society's involvement in building types, interior spatial relations, and modes of projection.

The Visual Dictionary of Interior Architecture and Design. **Graeme Brooker, Sally Stone, and Michael Coates. AVA Publishing, 2008.**
An overview of the terminology and language of the discipline of interior architecture and design.

Wow! Converted Spaces. **Julio Fajardo. Page One, 2008.**
A series of exciting case studies of interior spaces from across the world.

Journals

Abitare
www.abitare.it

Blueprint
www.blueprintmagazine.co.uk

Domus
www.domusweb.it

Frame
www.framemag.com

Icon Magazine
www.iconeye.com

Interior Design Magazine
www.interiordesign.net

Web resources

www.idec.org
The site of the American Interior Design Educators council.

www.ecia.net
The site for the European Council of Interior Architects offers lots of professional sources, case studies, books, and member details.

www.idea-edu.com
The home of the Interior Design/Interior Architecture Educators Association in Australia and New Zealand.

www.interioreducators.co.uk
The home page of IE, the association of UK-based interior educators, representing programs of interior architecture and design.

www.interiorsforumscotland.com/index.htm
The site for the Scottish Association of Interior Educators.

www.msa.mmu.ac.uk/continuity
A blog that discusses many aspects of design and architecture. Edited by academics, designers, and architects, it explores the connections between architecture and design of the past, present, and future.

www.thingsmagazine.net/index.htm
A strange magazine site that dazzles as well as illuminates lesser-known areas of design and aesthetics.

www.designaddict.com/index.cfm
A site that offers a rich source of objects, books, articles, and information.

bldgblog.blogspot.com
A great site that has also been turned into a book! Full of irreverent and obscure articles, projects, imagery, and ideas.

Glossary

Acoustics
The understanding and examination of sound and the aural qualities of a space. Within interior design the particular acoustic properties of a room can be controlled through the application of different materials, which affect the reverberation of noise within a space.

Applied texture
The visual identity and atmosphere of an interior space can be created through the use of specific materials, this is sometimes referred to as the surface finish. This final surface can be altered by the application of a new top layer. This is called an applied texture. This may be made from almost anything including: glass, metal, fabric, plastic, or timber.

Art deco
A style of design that was popular throughout Europe and North America in the early 1900s. Its aesthetic was characterized by crisp lines and geometric shapes.

Atrium
This term is commonly used to describe a covered interior space that usually has a glazed roof that allows sunlight and warmth to enter an interior. The space is usually at the center of an interior and will quite often have many different levels opening on to it.

Beam
The beam is a core component of a basic structural frame. It is a horizontal joist that is usually made from masonry, steel, or timber and is supported on either end by a column or load-bearing masonry. It is also known as a lintel, particularly when positioned over an opening in a wall.

Building regulations
The design and construction of buildings and interiors are all subject to specific regulations. These control issues such as planning, access, and health and safety within the building. Specific regulations such as DDA (Disability Discrimination Act) relate to access for all, and ensure that all forms of interior space can be safely and easily accessed.

Circulation
Movement through a space is often referred to as circulation. It denotes the methods that the users of a building will employ to access all areas of the interior. Circulation is often arranged as a series of routes, either horizontally through a building via walkways, corridors, and bridges, or vertically via stairs, ramps, elevators, and escalators.

Column
The column, along with the beam, forms the basic component of the structural system. It is the vertical element of construction and is usually made from masonry, steel, or timber.

Concept
A concept is an abstract idea that can act as the generator for the design of an interior. It can range from the pragmatic concerns of responding to a particular project or can be quite abstract.

Conservation
Conservation is the art of preserving existing structures, whether in their found form or by returning them back to their original state.

Context
In interior design, the context consists of the conditions surrounding the building and the original building itself. The context is the situation or environment into which the interior is positioned. These conditions may be in close proximity or far away and have a variety of impacts upon the new interior.

Design process
The design process is the method by which a new design is created and realized. It is often described and taught as a linear procedure, but it can also be a course of action that has different starting points and results.

Detail
The finalizing of a space and the application of materials and surfaces to an interior scheme is known as detailing. This often involves joinery, the application of materials, and sometimes prototyping, through the use of mock-ups and samples.

Elevation
An elevation is a drawing usually of an outside wall or façade of a building. It is a two-dimensional representation of a wall showing the position of windows, doors, and any other details of the building exterior.

Engineer
Structural, civil, mechanical, electrical, environmental, acoustic, and lighting engineers all have specialized knowledge and are often consulted by architects and designers in the design of buildings and interiors.

Ergonomics
The study of spatial relationships and proportions of the human body. This is exemplified by the *New Metric Handbook*, a book that catalogs these relationships and sets out the "standards" of ergonomic reasoning. Objects can also be described as "ergonomically" designed, in other words, it is obvious how they are used.

Form follows form
A term that particularly applies to the remodeling of the existing building. It is an approach to design that discusses how the nature of the original building has a direct impact upon, and relationship with, the new interior.

Form follows function
Form follows function is a phrase that was coined in the late nineteenth century. It is the modernist declaration that new buildings and interior spaces are determined by the functions that were going to take place inside of them.

Free plan
One of Le Corbusier's celebrated five points of architecture. The free plan is a system of design that uses a structure of columns, and thus removes the need for load-bearing walls. This creates a freedom and flexibility in the design of interiors, as the inside walls do not need to hold up the building, thus creating the opportunity for large and free-flowing spaces.

Function
The use of a space, either new or old, will often be referred to as the function of the space. Quite often function will also be referred to as "the program" of the interior, or the accommodation schedule for the new design.

Interior architecture
Interior architecture is the practice of remodeling existing buildings. As well as the robust reworking of a building, interior architecture often deals with complex structural, environmental, and servicing problems. It is sometimes referred to as adaptation, adaptive reuse, or remodeling.

Interior decoration

Interior decoration is the art of decorating inside spaces and rooms to impart a particular character and atmosphere to the room. It is often concerned with such issues as surface pattern, ornament, furniture, soft furnishings, and lighting.

Interior design

Interior design is an interdisciplinary practice concerned with the creation of a range of interior environments that articulate identity and atmosphere, through the manipulation of spatial volume, the placement of specific objects and furniture, and the treatment of surfaces.

Intervention

Intervention is a procedure that activates the potential or repressed meaning of a specific place. It truly works when the architectural response of the modifications draw all of their cues from the existing building.

Insertion

Insertion is the placement of a complete object within the confines of an existing building. It is a practice that establishes an intense relationship between the original building and the inserted element and yet allows the character of each to exist in a strong and independent manner.

Installation

Installation is the strategy of placing a series or group of related elements within the context of an existing building. This is a process that will heighten the awareness of an existing building without adversely affecting it.

Light

The manipulation of both natural and artificial light is an important consideration when designing interior space.

Listed building

When a building, an interior, or even a monument or bridge is considered to be of historic importance or of cultural significance, and therefore in need of protection from demolition or any insensitive changes, it is placed on a protected building list. The listing usually takes the form of a grading of importance from one through to three. Both the exterior and interior of a building may be listed.

Planning

The organization of an interior by arranging the rooms, spaces, and structure in a two-dimensional drawing.

Promenade

One of Le Corbusier's five-points of architecture, it is the modernist concept of continual movement through a building. This journey is also referred to as architectural promenade.

Raumplan (space plan)

Devised by the Viennese architect Adolf Loos, Raumplan (space plan) is best exemplified in the designs for the Müller and Moller houses in Prague and Vienna. The houses consist of a series of compact, enclosed, and intimately connected rooms. Movement between them was organized in a three-dimensional manner.

Ready-made

Art created from utilitarian everyday found objects, which would not normally be considered as art in their own right. The term ready-made was coined by the artist Marcel Duchamp, who created a series of objet d'art from such items as a bicycle wheel, a bottle rack, and a urinal.

Renovation

The process of renewing and updating a building. The function will remain the same and the structure is generally untouched, but the manner in which the building is used will be brought up to date. It is usually the services that require attention, especially the heating and sanitary systems.

Remodeling

Remodeling is the process of wholeheartedly altering a building. The function is the most obvious change, but other alterations may be made to the building such as its structure, circulation routes, and its orientation. Additions may be constructed and, conversely, certain areas may be demolished.

Restoration

Restoration is the process of returning the condition of the building to its original state, often involving using materials and techniques of the original period to ensure that the building appears as though it has just been constructed.

Section

At any point on the plan of a building, the designer may describe a line through the drawing and visualize a vertical cut through the spaces—this is called a section. Sections explain the volumes of the spaces and indicate the position of the walls, the floors, the roof, and other structural elements.

Sequence

Sequence is a term that describes the order of interior spaces that the designer intends the visitor to experience when on their journey through the interior.

Structure

Structure can be described as an assemblage of materials that will withstand the loads and forces to which they are subjected. Structure is one of the basic elements of the construction of space and can be made from many different materials, for example masonry, timber, and steel.

Sustainability

Within the design industry, sustainability refers to the sensible use of natural resources in the construction and use of a building or interior. It references materials that are used in a way that does not deplete them in an unnecessary or wasteful way. It also refers to the sourcing and use of methods of construction that do not contribute to climate change through the exhaustion of natural resources or their transport across the world.

Index

120BLOndo 164
3DStudio Max 54
6a architects 144, 148

A-Poc 86
Aaya Restaurant 200–202
acoustics 70–71, 151
adaptation 28–32, 73
Adjaye, David 116
advertising 48, 99
aesthetics 8, 52, 100, 131
affiliations 22, 180
Agence Andrée Putman 194–99
air quality 42
air-conditioning 45
American Institute of Interior
    Decorators 180
American Society of Interior
    Designers (ASID) 180
Amsterdam 186
analog methods 54
analytical sketches 55
Anne Fontaine boutique 199
Aparico + Fernàndez-Elorza 121
ApplePly 126
apprenticeship 20–21
ARB 23
Arca Architects 68
archaeology 34
Architectural Documentation
    Center 120
architecture 6, 10, 14, 17, 22,
    26, 35, 45, 54, 62, 80, 90,
    114–15, 134–35, 140, 180
Arribas, Alfredo 126
Arsenale 140
art deco 17
art school 21–22
Arts and Crafts 21
Asia 22, 180
Asia International Design Institute
    Association (AIDIA) 180
Athens Charter 33–34
Atkinson, Robert 17
atmosphere 12, 41, 44, 46, 49–50,
    53–54, 56, 70, 72, 88, 90,
    110, 112–13, 115–16, 128,
    131, 137, 148
Australia 175, 178, 181, 236
Austria 99, 124, 131
AutoCAD 54
autonomous interiors 62, 88–111,
    113, 134–51

balconies 49
Banq 125
Bar Ten 213
Barcelona 103, 154–56, 158
Barcelona chair 142
Basis Wien 124
Bauhaus 21–22
Behnisch Architekten 93
Beistegui apartment 180
Ben Kelly Design 153, 212–17
Berlin 50, 131
bespoke elements 46, 48, 149
Betsky, Aaron 140
Birkbeck College 78
Block, Klaus 25
Blue Spa 199
Bob Bob Ricard restaurant 207–8
books 17, 180
Boston 125
Bourellec brothers 142
Bourgeois, Francis 116
Bournemouth 203
Bouroullec, Ronan and Erwan 86,
    150
Bourriaud, Nicolas 39
brands 46, 62, 84, 88, 92, 108,
    110, 144, 147, 180
British Institute of Interior Design
    (BIID) 180

British Music Experience 245–46
brochures 48
Budapest 209
budgets 28, 71, 106, 144
building regulations 20, 23, 125,
    144
building reuse 6, 10, 23–25,
    27–29, 44–45, 70, 72
Burberry 241–42

Cabinet War Rooms 225–26
Café Bongo 52
CaixaForum 80
California 98
Callas Café 209
Camouflage exhibition 228
Canada 42
Canova, Antonio 76
Canteen 190
capital 29
Casson, Hugh 22
Casson Mann 153, 224–29
castings 40
Central School of Arts and Crafts
    21
certification 180
character 41, 46, 50, 64, 71, 73,
    112–13, 135
Chartered Society of Designers
    (CSD) 180
Chemetov, Huidobro and Allio 104
Chilean Pavilion 140
Churchill Museum 225
circulation 48, 74, 76, 121, 139
Cistercians 52
Civic Amenities Act 35
cladding 50, 100, 125, 135, 147
Click 3X LA 172
climate 42, 114
Clive Wilkinson Architects 71, 152,
    218–23
Coates, Nigel 52
Codman, Ogden 17
Colefax, Sibyl 17
collaboration 27, 42
collage 39, 54
Collins, David 152
Cologne 137
Comme des Garçons 110
Commerzbank 126
commodity 10
communication 54–59, 84,
    142–44, 148
community design 63
computers 23, 57, 80, 112
conceptual sketches 55
Concertgebouw 186–87
conservation 10, 25–27, 32–35
Constable, John 66
construction drawings 58
contractors 28
Coop Himmelb(l)au 99
Le Corbusier 22, 180
Cordiere exhibition space 140
Corian 86
costs 20, 23
Crate House 91
Cuines Santa-Caterina 158
Culver City 169
curators 140
curriculum 21
Czech Republic 50

Daily Express Building 178
David Archer Architects 152,
    200–205
David Collins Studio 206–11
decoration 6, 10–11, 14, 17,
    22–23, 66
Denmark 116
Desenfans, Noël 116

details 55, 58, 69, 110, 112–13,
    115, 134
diplomas 22
domestic interiors 12, 14
Dover Street market 110
Draper, Dorothy 17
drawing 23, 54–56, 58
Droog Design 108
Duchamp, Marcel 25, 38
Dulwich Picture Gallery 116

Edelma 243
education 6, 20–24, 63
elevations 58, 82
elevators 48–49
Eliden 192
emissions 42
Emporio Armani 52
energy consumption 42–43
engineers 27
England 68
environment 12, 23, 44–45, 49
ergonomics 49, 62, 70, 100, 142
Europe 180
Evans, Robin 54
events 180
exhibitions 12, 26–27, 76, 88, 94,
    103–4, 116, 126, 135–37,
    140, 147, 180

fashion 8, 26, 86, 108, 110
Fashion Institute of Technology 22
Fendi 230–33
finishes 20, 23, 49–50, 112–13
firmness 10
fittings 48
fixings 48
Fleet Street 178
flooring 48
FNP Architekten 144
form 34, 45, 49, 54, 56, 60, 112,
    115, 134
formZ 54
Foster + Partners 50
Foster, Norman 126
found objects 25, 36–41, 48, 147
France 197, 199, 230
Frankfurt 126
Fujimoto, Sou 151
Fuksas, Doriana and Massimiliano
    52
function 8, 10, 60, 62, 112, 124,
    126
furniture 12, 14, 17, 27, 48–49, 54,
    58, 106, 122, 135, 142

galleries 12, 38, 62–63, 76, 82,
    91, 94, 116, 122, 137
Gamble, James 128
GAS Eatery and Supplies 236
Gensler 152, 238–43
Germany 42, 70, 126, 131, 137,
    144, 199
Gherkin 142
Glasgow 213
Glenlyon church 175–77
global warming 42
Golden Age of Couture 248
Gordon Square 78, 80
graffiti 50
Graft Lab 131
Grand Central Station 228
Grand Projects 104
graphics 8, 27, 180
gray water 44
Graz 131
Great Expectations 228
Groninger Museum 136
Guangdong Company 43
Guangzhou 43
guerrilla stores 110
guilds 20
Gymbox Covent Garden 214

The Haçienda 212–14
Hakuhodo Head Office 242
Hamburg Chamber of Commerce
    92–94
Haworth Tompkins 36–38, 73
health spaces 180
heating systems 42, 44
Herter brothers 17
Herzog & de Meuron 62, 80
history 11, 14–20, 23–24, 26, 30,
    33, 36, 50, 60, 62, 64, 115
home 60, 63, 66–69, 90–91, 151
Hong Kong 52
Horus Capital 228
Hotel Bayerischer Hof Spa 199
Hotel OMM 154–56
hotels 12, 23
House 40
Howell, Bill 72
Hungary 209
hygiene 131

identity 12, 35, 45–46, 49–50, 52,
    54, 70, 72, 84, 88, 92, 99,
    108, 126, 128, 131, 134, 148
Imperial War Museum 228
Incorporated Institute of British
    Decorators (IIBD) 180
industry 8, 27, 52, 54, 62, 70–71,
    78, 90, 180
Ink Bar 203–4
installations 6, 10, 26, 32, 90, 93,
    110, 116, 131
insulation 42, 44, 70
interior architecture 6, 11, 14, 17,
    22–23, 28, 77
interior decoration 6, 10–11, 14, 23
interior design role 6, 8–13, 180
International Energy Agency 42
International Federation of Interior
    Designers/Architects (ifilDA)
    180
Isarn restaurant 205
Italy 32, 34, 108, 110, 144, 235

Jamie Fobert Architects 142
Japan 52, 151, 242
Jigsaw Headquarters 171
Johan menswear 131
John Luce Company 163
Joyn Table 143
juxtaposition 41, 46, 52, 110, 140

Kawakubo, Rei 110
Kelly, Ben 25
Klein, Calvin 52
KMS Design Agency 70
knowledge 60, 63, 78–83, 104–7
Kolumba Art Museum 137
Koolhaas, Rem 84
Korea 192
Kumakura 151
Kunsthalcafé 185
Kvadrat 116, 150

labor 29
Laetitia and Sebastian House 181
Lan, David 73
land art 26
Land Design Studio 153, 244–49
laws 35, 144
layout 58
Lazzarini Pickering Architetti 152,
    230–37
legislation 6, 180
Lehrer Architects 98
leisure 26, 180
Levitt Bernstein Architects 100
libraries 63, 71, 78, 80, 106, 147
light 12, 17, 27, 34, 46, 48–49, 52,
    56, 66–68, 71, 76, 78–79, 84,
    90, 98, 112–13, 115–19, 124,
    131, 133, 136–39
Lincoln's Inn Fields 66

listed structures 32
London 21, 36, 40, 62, 66–67, 71–72, 77–78, 99–100, 110, 116, 142, 148, 178, 190, 200, 205, 207, 214, 225, 228, 241, 243, 245, 248–49
The London NYC 210
London Stock Exchange 239–40
Loos, Adolf 178
Los Angeles 98, 171, 219, 221, 223
LOT-EK 40, 90
Lotte Department Store 192
Lucca Cathedral Museum 32
Lynx Architects 70

Maastricht 182
Machado, Rodolfo 24
McInnes Usher McKnight Architects (MUMA) 128
McQueen, Alexander 86
Madrid 80, 120, 157
makeover shows 6, 66
Manchester 100, 103, 139, 212
Manchester School of Architecture 103
Manchester School of Art 21
Mandarina Duck 108
Manhattan 86, 90
Mann, Casson 25
Massachusetts University 91
materials 12, 20, 22–23, 43–44, 48–50, 52–53, 55–56, 60, 68–69, 71, 84, 86, 112, 114–15, 128, 131, 148
mausoleums 116
Melbourne 178, 181, 236
Merkx + Girod 152, 182–87
meshes 52, 74
mezzanines 66, 142
Milan 110
Millennium Dome 249
minimalism 50, 131, 178
Mitterand, François 104
Miyake, Issey 86
modeling 57, 80
models 54, 57–58, 76, 140
modernism 39, 134, 141, 178
monuments 32–33
Morecambe 68
Morgan's Hotel 195–96
Morris, William 128
Morton Duplex 90
Moscow 227–28
Mother 99
movie theaters 78–79
Multiplicity 153, 174–81
Munich 70, 199
Museo Gipsoteca Possagno 76
Museum Quarter 124
museums 12, 27, 39, 63, 78, 104, 116, 128, 136

narrative 50, 116
National Historic Preservation Act 35
neoclassicism 100, 120
Netherlands 136, 182, 185–86
New Order 118
New York 22, 40, 71, 84, 86, 90, 122, 189, 195, 210, 228
New York School of Interior Design 22
Next Generation House 151
nitrous oxide 42
North Tile 150
Nottingham School of Art 21
Novy Dvur Monastery 50, 52

O2 arena 245
objects 113, 120–23, 140–43
off-the-peg items 38, 40, 46
Office dA 106, 125–26

offices 12, 20, 26, 63, 82, 94, 98–99, 116, 139, 142
oki-ni 148–49
OMA 84
Omaha 163–64
OMI Architects 139
orientation 44, 64, 67
orthogonal drawings 58

painting 20, 22, 26, 54
Palladio, Andrea 144
Pallotta TeamWorks 219–20
Paperfish 223
Paris 86, 108, 180, 197, 199, 230, 248
Paris Natural History Museum 104
Parsons School of Design 22
passive systems 44, 115
Passivhaus 42
patrons 14
pattern 12, 27
Pawson, John 50, 52, 131
Pearl River Tower 42
Pellegrini, Pietro Carlo 32
Photoshop 54
plane 113, 124–27, 144–47
planning laws 20
plans 58
plastics 52, 86, 112
Playzone 249
pollution 42
portfolios 152–249
Positano 235
postmodernism 39
postgraduates 6, 23
Poulson Kjeldseth Advertising 166
Poynter, Edward 128
practitioners 6, 17, 21
Prada 84
presentation 57–58
preservation 26, 32–35
principles 6
product design 27
professional organizations 180
proportion 52
public buildings 12
public works 32
Pugh + Scarpa 152, 168–73
Putman, Andrée 152, 194–99

qualifications 20, 23

R-2000 42
rain 44
Ranalli, George 90
Randy Brown Architects 152, 160–67
ready-made items 38
Recycled Architecture Unit 103
recycling 44
registers 32, 106
Reichstag 50
remixing 39
remodeling 11, 23–24, 28, 30, 32–34, 36, 40, 44, 62, 64, 66–68, 80, 100, 124, 139, 144, 180
Renaissance 144
renovation 38
representation 54–59
responsive interiors 62, 64, 66–87, 111, 114–33
restaurants 12, 82, 86, 94, 125, 131
restoration 26, 32–35
retail 12, 23, 26, 60, 62–63, 84–88, 108–11, 122, 135, 141, 147–48, 180
reuse 6, 10, 23–25, 27–28, 36, 39, 41, 44–45, 70, 72–73, 78, 106
reworking 28
Rheinland-Pfalz 144
Rhino software 126

Rhode Island School of Design 106
RIBA 23
Richmond warehouse 178
Rohe, Mies van der 142
Rotterdam 185
Roy, Lindy 122
Royal College of Art 22
Royal Court Theatre 36–38
Royal Exchange Theatre 100
Russia 227–28

St Mary Axe 142
St Paul's Church Bow 100, 102
sampling 39
Santa Monica 172
Saskatchewan House 42
Savile Row 148
Saville, Peter 116, 118
scale 34, 54, 69, 76, 106
Scamozzi, Vincenzo 144
Scarpa, Carlo 34, 76
scenic painting 17, 26
sculpture 40, 49, 76, 86, 90
Selexyz Dominicanen bookstore 182–84
Seoul 192
set design 27, 116, 144
Seti 66
Shaw, D.E. 71
sheathing surfaces 50
Shoreditch 116
Silverlake 98
Silvestrin, Claudio 50, 131
Silvetti, Jorge 32
Simon Conder Associates 67
simulation 54
Siobhan Davies dance school 77
Sioux City 166
sketch models 54, 57, 76
sketches 23, 55
Skidmore Owings Merrill LLP 43
Soane, John 66–67, 116
soft furnishings 12
software 54, 126
SoHo 84
Solà-Morales, Ignasi de 30
solar gain 64
Le Spa Guerlain 197–98
Spain 80, 120, 154–58
stage sets 144, 180
staircases 48–49, 71, 112, 118, 122
Stanislavski Museolobby 227
Starck, Philippe 136
Stella McCartney headquarters 189
Steven Holl Architects 71
Stockholm 150
strategy 60, 62, 64–111
structure 10, 56, 60, 64, 96, 100, 115
suffragettes 14
sulfur dioxide 42
surface 49–53, 113, 128–33, 148–49
Surface Architects 78, 80
surrealism 180
sustainability 10, 23, 26, 42–45
Sweden 150

tactics 60, 112–51
Tarruella & Lopez 153–59
Task 13 42
Tate Modern 62
TBWA/Chiat/Day 221
Teatro Olimpico 144
technology 30, 64, 71, 90
Terry, Emilio 180
textiles 17, 52, 116, 150–51
texture 6, 50
theaters 23, 27, 63, 72–74, 82, 100, 116, 144
three-dimensional drawings 56

Tokyo 52, 242
trades 20
tradition 115, 134, 142
training 21–22, 24
Turner, J.M.W. 66
Turner Prize 40
Turrell, James 116

undergraduates 6
United Kingdom (UK) 22–23, 35, 42, 139, 180, 190, 200, 203, 205, 207, 212–14, 225, 228, 239, 241, 243, 245, 248–49
United States (US) 22, 35, 163–64, 166, 169, 171–72, 180, 189, 195, 210, 219, 221, 223, 228
Universal Design Studio 152, 188–93
Universitat Politècnica de Catalunya 103
upholstery 14, 17, 20, 26

Vectorworks 54
Veils 116
Venice Architectural Biennale 140
ventilation 42, 44, 80
vernacular architecture 32, 45, 114, 144
Vialis Shoes 157
Vicenza 144
Victoria 175
Victoria and Albert Museum 128, 248
Victorians 116
Vienna 99, 124
Viktor & Rolf 110
Villa 235
Vitra 122, 142
Vitruvius 10
volume 12, 54, 56, 58, 67, 76, 88

Wall Works 116
wallpaper 52
walls 50, 58, 134, 142, 144, 150
weather 67, 144
weaving 22
Webb, Philip 128
Wexler, Alex 91
Wharton, Edith 17
White Cube 90
Whiteread, Rachel 39–40
Wigglesworth, Sarah 77
windows 42, 44, 58, 64, 69, 71, 76, 131
Wolfe, Elsie de 17, 21
Women's Library 80
work 60, 63, 70–71, 92–99, 180
World War II 50, 180
Wright & Wright Architects 80

Xap Corporation 169–70

York & Sawyer 106
Young Vic 72–74
YouTube 80

Zero Energy Buildings 42
Zumthor, Peter 137

Credits

Graeme Brooker would like to thank: Shelley McNulty and Howard Cooper (MMU ID team) for their support; Fredo Viola, Ben Evans, Sylvain Rebut-Minotti, and Jasper Wilkinson for their constitution; Mido El-Alfy and Finn Salter for driving safely; and Claire for her strength.

Sally Stone would like to thank: Eamonn Canniffe for his encouragement; Reuben, Ivan, and Agnes for their tolerance; and Dominic for his perspicacity and assiduousness.

Graeme and Sally would like to thank: the Manchester interior design students for their drawings, all the photographers and designers who have given permission for their work to be used, and Jane Roe for her patience and forbearance during the production of the book.

Photography credits

3: Andi Albert Photographie. 7: Graeme Brooker (GB). 8: Design by Softroom and the Virgin Atlantic Design Team; photo by Richard Davies. 9 (left top and bottom): GB. Right © Givenchy. Courtesy Jamie Fobert Architects. 10: Courtesy Diller Scofidio +Renfro. 13: Killian O'Sullivan of Light Room Photography. Courtesy Surface Architects. 14: © Pawel Libera/Corbis. 15: © Ludovic Maisant/Corbis. 16: Albertina, Vienna. 19: © Martin Jones/Arcaid/Corbis. 20. Rachel Vallance. 21. Michaela O'Hare. 22. Jo Matssonn. 25: Courtesy Ben Kelly Design. 26: Paul Tahon and R & E Bouroullec. 27: GB. 29-31: Courtesy Richard Murphy Architects. 33: (top) Courtesy London Metropolitan Archive (bottom) David Grandorge. 34: GB. 35: © Richard Bryant/Arcaid/Corbis. 36: (top) Antoni Malinowski; (bottom) Andy Chopping. 37: Haworth Tompkins. 38: Andy Chopping. 39: © Richard Lewis/epa/Corbis. 40: Courtesy Pugh + Scarpa. 43: © Brecelj Bojan/Corbis Sygma. 44: © Construction Photography/Corbis. 45: Courtesy Wright & Wright Architects. 46 David Grandorge. Courtesy 6a architects. 47 (top): GB. 47 (bottom): © Richard Bryant/Arcaid/Corbis. 48: Courtesy Ben Kelly Design. 51: Richard Davies. 52: GB. 53 (top left): Paul Tahon and R & E Bouroullec. 53 (bottom): Courtesy Architecture Research Office (ARO). 55 (left): Samantha Hart (right) Alex Johnson. 56 (top left): Courtesy 6a Architects (mid left): Kara Latham (right); Courtesy propellor z (bottom): Bourrellec Brothers. 57: Samantha Hart. 58: Jo Matssonn. 59 (top): Dave Smith (bottom): Courtesy OMI Architects. 61: GB. 63: GB. 65: © Chris Gascoigne/View. 66-67: Courtesy Simon Conder Associates. 68: © Chris Gascoigne/View. 70: © Victor S. Brigola/Artur/View. 72 (top) and 73 (top and middle): Haworth Tompkins. 72 (bottom) and 73 (bottom): Philip Vile. 74-75: Haworth Tompkins. 76-77: GB. 78-81: Courtesy Wright & Wright Architects. 82-83: Courtesy Greg Epps. 84-85: Morgane Le Gall. 86-87: Frank Oudeman. 89: © Wouter VandenBrink. 91: © Allan Wexler. 92-97: Courtesy Behnisch Architekten. 98: Courtesy Lehrer Architects. 99: Adrian Wilson. Supplied by C.W.A. 100-102: GB. 103: Sally Stone. 104-105: GB. 106-107: John Horner Photography. 109: © Wouter VandenBrink. 110-111: Andrea Martiradonna. 112: Ben Kelly Design. 114: GB. 117: © Richard Bryant/Arcaid/Corbis. 118-119: Ed Reeves. Courtesy of Kvadrat. 120-121: © Roland Halbe/artur images. 122-123: GB. 124: Sally Stone. 125-126: John Horner Photography. 127: Courtesy Alfredo Arribas. 128-129: Alan Williams Photography. 130: GB. 132-133: Andi Albert Photographie. 135: GB. 136 Courtesy Philippe Starck. 137. Sally Stone. 138-139: Courtesy OMI Architects. 140-141: GB. 142: © Dennis Gilbert/View. 143: © Vitra. Supplied by Bouroullec Brothers. 145: Courtesy FNP Architekten. 146-147: David Grandorge. 148: David Grandorge. 149: Sketch by 6a Architects. 149 (bottom) and 150-151: Paul Tahon and R & E Bouroullec. 155-156: Rafael Vargas. 157: Luis Asin. 158-159: Eugeni Pons. 160-167: Courtesy Randy Brown Architects. 169-170: Benny Chan. 171-173: Marvin Rand. 174-179: Emma Cross. 180-181: Courtesy Multiplicity. 182-185: Roos Aldershoff. 186-187: Courtesy Merkx + Girod. 188-189 and 192-193: Courtesy Universal Design Studio. 190-191: Simon Phipps. 194-199: Eric Laignel. 201-204: Keith Collie. 205: Joakim Blockström. 206-211: Courtesy David Collins Studio. 212-217: Courtesy Ben Kelly Design. 218-223: © Fotoworks. 224-229: Courtesy Casson Mann. 230-237: Courtesy Lazzarini Pickering Architetti. 238-243: Courtesy Gensler. 244-249: Courtesy Land Design Studio.